THE FAMILY STORY

IN THE 1960's

Anne W Ellis

THE FAMILY STORY
IN THE 1960's

ARCHON BOOKS & CLIVE BINGLEY

FIRST PUBLISHED 1970 BY CLIVE BINGLEY LTD
THIS EDITION SIMULTANEOUSLY PUBLISHED IN THE USA
BY ARCHON BOOKS, THE SHOE STRING PRESS INC,
995 SHERMAN AVENUE, HAMDEN, CONNECTICUT 06514
PRINTED IN GREAT BRITAIN
COPYRIGHT © ANNE W ELLIS 1970
ALL RIGHTS RESERVED
208 00881 0

CONTENTS

		page
INTRODUCTION		7
chapter one:	The evolution of the family story	9
chapter two:	Relationships inside and outside the family	21
chapter three:	Everyday life of the 1960's reflected in the family story	37
chapter four:	Problems	58
chapter five:	Conclusion	75
SOURCES OF INFORMATION		81
FAMILY STORIES OF THE 1960'S		86
INDEX		95

INTRODUCTION

The germ of the idea for this book can be traced to a talk: *The development of the family story*, which I gave at a Scottish County Library Circle Weekend School at Arbroath in 1958. There was, however, no idea then of pursuing the topic to the extent that the results would emerge in book form. The aims of this short book are to arouse in the reader at least a fraction of the enthusiasm and pleasure that I have derived from family stories, whatever their failings, since my own childhood; to attempt in so far as it is possible at this stage in time, to comment on trends in the family stories published in the 1960's; and lastly, to show very tentatively the international nature of the family story during the same decade. This is an attempt to capture a picture of family life in the 1960's as reflected in children's books of the period, from three main angles: human relationships; everyday life; and problems facing the characters. It is hoped that this study will prove of immediate interest for its coverage in some detail of a small section of the map of children's literature, and of future interest for its mention of at least some material which may eventually be completely forgotten. It must be stressed that books mentioned and listed constitute an entirely personal choice, and that all books mentioned have been read by me. The books used for this survey are generally those written for children of about ten years of age upwards, although occasional exceptions may be found. It should be pointed out that the material used is mainly that available in British editions during the 1960's, although sometimes it may have been available earlier in the countries of origin.

This book has only been achieved with the very practical help and encouragement of my husband, Alec, who has also been a severe mentor. His invaluable assistance with the preparation of the bibliographies considerably reduced the task. Acknowledgments must be gratefully made to the numerous authors and publishers, without whose works this book would never have been written. Grateful thanks are also due to Vincent Roper FLA, who was responsible for selecting the collection of children's books for the Childwall Branch of Liverpool Public Libraries opened in 1968. His discerning selection simplified the problem of obtaining access to both British material and outstanding works from the Commonwealth, the United States, and other countries.

ANNE W ELLIS

Childwall, Liverpool
June 1969

8

chapter one

THE EVOLUTION OF THE FAMILY STORY

Since John Newbery made literary history in 1744 with his production of *A little pretty pocket book*, recognised as one of the first children's books designed entirely to give children pleasure, there has been an incessant conflict between instruction and entertainment in children's literature. This conflict is still evident today, and can be traced clearly in the history of the family story, which originally came into existence as the 'moral tale', with works such as *Early lessons*, 1801, by Maria Edgeworth; *Sandford and Merton*, 1783-89, by Thomas Day; or *The history of the Fairchild family*, 1818-47, by Mrs Martha Mary Sherwood. *Holiday House*, by Catherine Sinclair, was an early family story with the object of entertainment, although the present day adult reader may find parts of the book all too pious, and may take exception to descriptions such as the death bed of Frank.

Contributions to the family story were made in the second half of the nineteenth century by three outstanding women writers: Charlotte M Yonge, Mrs Juliana Horatia Ewing and Mrs Mary Louisa Molesworth. According to F J Harvey Darton in *Children's books in England*, Miss Yonge 'intensified the home interest until it became almost

9

1*

exciting ' in works for older girls, which include *The heir of Redclyffe*, 1853, and *The daisy chain*, 1856. In her books for girls, Miss Yonge aimed not only at giving pleasure, but also at exerting a moral influence based on her own strong Tractarian beliefs.

Mrs Ewing deserves to be remembered for her gentle family stories which include *Six to sixteen*, 1875, and *Mary's meadow*, 1886, while the prolific Mrs Molesworth wrote family stories for a wide age group, which include the now almost forgotten *Carrots*, 1876, and *The adventures of Herr Baby*, 1881. A few of Mrs Molesworth's family fantasies which are still read and enjoyed over seventy years after their original publication include *The cuckoo clock*, 1877, and *The carved lions*, 1895. Other nineteenth century family stories written to give children pleasure and reprinted today include *Castle Blair*, 1877, by Flora Shaw and *The gentle heritage*, 1893, by Frances Crompton. In the nineteenth century the rigidly moral type of family story was provided by writers of the calibre of either Mary Louisa Charlesworth or Hesba Stretton, whose work is now mainly of historical interest. The attitudes propagated by a writer like Miss Charlesworth in *Ministering children*, 1854, were totally alien to children of the 1960's growing up in a welfare state.

A more lasting contribution to the family story was made by American writers of international repute, and particularly by Louisa M Alcott, who consolidated the work of earlier American writers of domestic fiction, now forgotten by all but the literary historian. Louisa M Alcott is best known for the four volumes about the March family, of which *Little women*, 1868, is probably the most popular; but of her other numerous books for girls, *An old-fashioned girl*, 1870, *Eight cousins*, 1874, its sequel *Rose in bloom*, 1876 and *Under the lilacs*, 1878, are still readable today. Louisa M Alcott was successful in her day because she wrote about entirely ordinary families, neither impossibly perfect nor obtrusively moral, neither incredibly exciting nor tediously dull. She herself described *Little women* as ' not a bit sensational, but simple and true, for we really lived most of it, and if it succeeds, that will be the reason for it '. There can be no doubt that it succeeded.

Other American writers of the nineteenth century, whose books were read on both sides of the Atlantic, included Martha Finley (or

Farquharson), Elizabeth Wetherell, Susan Coolidge and Maria
Susanna Cummins. Some of the works of Susan Coolidge and Elizabeth Wetherell are enjoyed today: Susan Coolidge's *What Katy did*,
1872, and *What Katy did at school*, 1873, usually remain unaltered,
while Elizabeth Wetherell's *The wide, wide world*, originally published in 1851, was satisfactorily abridged in 1950 by Joyce Lankester
Brisley, who succeeded in preserving the essence of the story without
the now intolerable moralising and tearfulness of the original version.
Martha Finley's books about Elsie Dinsmore, twenty eight of which
appeared from 1867 onwards, were widely read, but have not lasted.
Their excessive sentimentality was in the mood of their period, but
is alien to a later generation. Another American story adopted by
some British children was *The lamplighter*, 1854, by Maria Susanna
Cummins. Mrs Frances Hodgson Burnett emigrated from England
to America, and her essentially English story, *Little Lord Fauntleroy*,
was published in 1886. It enjoyed an incredible popularity in its
day, is still in print, and was the source of inspiration for *The real
game*, by Rosemary Weir, published in 1965. Two other books, by
Mrs Frances Hodgson Burnett, less popular than *Little Lord Fauntleroy* when published, but more popular in the 1960's, were *A little
princess*, 1905, and *The secret garden*, 1911.

From Europe there has been a greater contribution to fields of
fantasy and high adventure than to the sometimes more quiet and
gentle field of family life. One of the earliest European contributions
to the story of domestic life may have been the much loved *Heidi*,
1880, by a Swiss, Johanna Spyri, which Brian Alderson, in his translation of Bettina Hürlimann's *Three centuries of children's books in
Europe*, considered as ' the export that has lasted the best, but her
appeal and influence have been greater in America than in Britain '.
Even *Heidi* is not strictly a family story, but a compelling tale of
homesickness. *Les malheurs de Sophie*, 1864, by the French Comtesse de Ségur was a bestseller in its day, but is unlikely to be known
to British children now.

By the early twentieth century, Edith Nesbit was creating her
unique Psammead, the Phoenix, and the Mouldiwarp for her remarkable family fantasies, in which morals if inserted at all, are discreetly
unobtrusive. Family fantasies with the imaginative qualities of *The*

carved lions, by Mrs Molesworth, or *The phoenix and the carpet*, 1904, by E Nesbit might have been read by children in the 1960's, but the highly moral *Sandford and Merton* or *The history of the Fairchild family* were only likely to be examined by the student of literary history.

The golden period of E Nesbit was followed by dormant years in the development of the family story, but by the 1930's Arthur Ransome was writing stories, not only to give children pleasure, but also to give them a mass of information about sailing and camping. In *Written for children*, John Rowe Townsend wrote that ' in the early 1930's Arthur Ransome's *Swallows and Amazons* series gave a new direction to English children's writing and also gave it a new, or revived, seriousness after years of casual commercialism '. Although John Rowe Townsend was severely critical of Arthur Ransome's work, he had to agree that 'Ransome wrote without condescension about the real lives of real children'. Noel Streatfeild's readable, entertaining stories, the earliest of which were written in the 1930's, also provide accurate factual detail, whether about child actors, skating, tennis or filming in Hollywood. Until the 1930's the family story had been set almost exclusively in the middle class family, partly because in real life, children of middle class background were more likely to have access to books, in spite of the efforts made from the middle of the nineteenth century, both through education acts and public libraries acts, to improve the literacy of working class children. Eleanor Graham wrote scathingly in *The junior bookshelf*, July 1944, of the ' familiar pre-war formula for a " good modern story "—to get rid of the parents, divorce the children from home surroundings and influence, and in an atmosphere of artificial freedom, to project them into a succession of thrilling adventures, very unlikely to occur in real life '. Stories were invariably written by writers of middle class background, even in the case of Eve Garnett, who could hardly have anticipated the literary history she was making when *The family from One End Street* was published in 1937. Nearly every relevant book or bibliography which includes family stories mentions *The family from One End Street*, no matter what other material is included or excluded. More than thirty years later, much of the detail is out of date on matters relating to the cinema, to grammar school or to laundering. Its reflected attitudes of middle class superiority and of condescension are no longer officially acceptable, but, when *The family from One End Street* was originally published, it was the first outstanding story about an English working class family in the 1930's. There is no question of it being a book written to give pleasure: it was written with a dedicated sense of social purpose. Brian Doyle pointed out in *The who's who of children's literature* that 'in the late 1930's it made children realise that not all their contemporaries had nurseries, or attended boarding schools'. *The family from One End Street* was, in the 1930's, recognisable reality for a neglected group of readers. No more general attempt to cater for this large group was made until the 1950's, when a movement began which gained momentum in the 1960's. Today, the two extremes of instruction and entertainment commonly emerge, either in stories with an almost too heavily laboured working class setting, like *A pair of Jesus-boots* by Sylvia Sherry, or in fantasies with a family setting of the outstanding quality of *Earthfasts* by William Mayne, or *Elidor* by Alan Garner.

In the 1930's the European tendency almost to ignore family life in their literature continued. Two of the few examples of the period eventually available in English translations are not strictly family stories: the 'Mimff' books by H J Kaeser or *Timpetill*, by Swiss Manfred Michael. The books of neither author reached British children until more than twelve years after their original publication.

In Britain, the 1940's was a barren period in the development of the family story, apart from the various popular adventure series by Enid Blyton; but in America a lasting contribution to the *genre* was made by both Elizabeth Enright and Eleanor Estes, whose books were gradually made available in British editions in the 1950's and 1960's. Both writers received recognition for their work with awards of the Newbery medal. Although Elizabeth Enright received the Newbery medal for *Thimble summer,* in Britain she is probably best loved for *The Saturdays* and its sequels about the Melendy family. Eleanor Estes is remembered for her Pye and Moffat families, whose activities are faithfully recorded in *Ginger Pye*, in *Pinky Pye* and in *The Moffats* and its sequels.

By the 1960's there was a welcome tendency for American, European and Commonwealth material to be more speedily available than before in British editions. The works of Americans Robert Burch, Mrs E L Konigsburg and Joseph Krumgold were available in British editions within a few years of original publication, rather than taking a decade as was the case with most of the books of Elizabeth Enright and Eleanor Estes. From the 1950's, the University of London Press pioneered the production of English translations of award winning European material by Paul Jacques Bonzon, Harry Kullman, A Rutgers Van der Loeff and others. Other publishers increased their numbers of translations with the result that by the 1960's some outstanding European material was available in Britain. There were still very few purely family stories, but the 1950's will be remembered for *The girl from nowhere,* by German Hertha von Gebhardt; *Rasmus and the tramp,* by Swedish Astrid Lindgren; and *Za the truffle boy,* by Italian Angela Latini. In the 1960's *Kersti,* by Norwegian Babbis Friis was a rare example of a European family story complete with mother and father, a mischievous brother and a new baby as well as Kersti. The parentless pattern, on the other hand, was followed by both Swedish Maria Gripe in *Pappa Pellerin's daughter* and by Italian Renée Reggiani in *The adventures of five children and a dog.*

The 1950's and 1960's also showed an increase in the amount of material available to British children from various parts of the Commonwealth. In 'The present state of children's literature ', an article in *Wilson library bulletin,* October 1968, John Rowe Townsend wrote that ' a welcome transfusion has come from Australian writers ' to stories of contemporary life. Distinguished writers from Australia included H F Brinsmead, Ivan Southall and Eleanor Spence. Nan Chauncy depicted life in Tasmania, while both Andrew Salkey and C Everard Palmer gave vivid details of Jamaica. P H Nortje gave a not always sympathetic account of South African life, and Sita Rathnamal wrote a most moving picture of an Indian girl's life.

From all parts of the world, whatever aims are intended or achieved, come numerous family stories which centre around either the difficulties of family relationships, or the multifarious types of problem which are liable to arise within any family unit. The purpose of this study is to attempt to assess how current family stories succeed in giving realistic details of relationships both inside and outside the family, of family life and of family problems in the 1960's.

The chronological development of family stories as a specific branch of children's literature has been very briefly outlined, but it is also essential to consider some of the special characteristics of the family stories of the eighteenth and nineteenth centuries which have subsequently influenced the development of the family story in the twentieth century. Recurring characteristics, with exceptions, included enormous families, absent parents, reasonably affluent middle class backgrounds, faithful family servants, separate lives of parents and children. There are striking contrasts, not only of period, between earlier and recent family stories.

A well accepted criterion of a good children's book is that it should reflect desirable attitudes. This standard was upheld in family stories of the eighteenth and nineteenth centuries, with their strong moral overtones which often formed an essential part of the story. This is true of Maria Edgeworth's work and was perfectly demonstrated in *The purple jar*, in which Rosamund prefers the beautiful purple jar in the chemist's shop to a pair of new shoes and is bitterly disappointed over her rash choice. More harrowing incidents were used to inculcate morals by Mrs Sherwood, and whatever incidents are forgotten, readers are likely to remember the occasion in *The history of the Fairchild family* when the father takes his children to inspect a body on a gibbet. This outing provided an excellent opportunity for an appropriate homily. The moral issues of earlier periods were superseded in the 1960's by pressing contemporary issues over class, colour and creed, to mention only three topics on which desirable attitudes need to be encouraged. In a more leisurely age, writers for an essentially middle class audience could conveniently concentrate on more abstract virtues while ignoring glaring social inequalities. Today, it might be thought that writers for children should be encouraging responsible attitudes to more concrete issues, but in many cases they are still politely ignoring them, as Janet A Hill maintained in her article: 'A minority view', which appeared in *Children's book news*, May-June 1967. It could be argued that eighteenth and nineteenth century writers reflected the attitudes of their periods, but paid less attention to reflecting life in all walks of society, and that today the reverse is more true.

In earlier family stories, families were usually comfortably off and looked after by a battery of servants. In her introduction to *Victorian tales for girls,* 1947, Marghanita Laski stated that Victorian family stories give a picture of Victorian family life with the following details: a large family of seven or eight living in a spacious house, which invariably has a nursery; a father of professional upper middle class standing; self contained family life, and a degree of security which seems unbelievable to a later generation. Family stories of the period also, in Marghanita Laski's opinion reflected problems which were peculiar to the Victorian period: the miseries of children separated from their Empire-building parents; the sufferings of children left in the care of ignorant and unkind servants. The death of parents is a problem not peculiar to any one period. The tradition of middle class setting has persisted in spite of the altered scene in real life, and provokes comment by several writers, including Frank Eyre, who says, in *Twentieth century children's books,* that most stories ' are written for, or about, the children of upper middle class families, and the quite extraordinary snobbishness betrayed in many of them (especially in that now considerable group known as " pony stories ") is lamentable '. Faithful family retainers, although diminished in number in the 1960's, still played a conspicuous part in a limited number of books as different one from another as *Requiem for a princess,* by Ruth M Arthur; *Peter's room,* by Antonia Forest; or *The children on the top floor,* by Noel Streatfeild.

The increase in the number of stories with lower middle class or working class backgrounds, however, was a healthy indication that family stories in the 1960's were attempting to reflect real life and not some ideal fantasy world. This change can be attributed partly to the social upheavals of the twentieth century, and also to a move on the part of authors to provide stories with realistic backgrounds for a wider audience of children. In *Bookbird,* no 3, 1968, the Swedish author Eva von Zweigbergk deplored the lack of children's books with an industrial environment, and suggested that ' it takes 10 to 15 years before a new theme can be accepted '. British children's books give the impression that it takes even longer for a new theme to be absorbed. As early as 1938 Eleanor Graham wrote *The children who lived in a barn* as an alternative to the unrealistic family stories of the period. Authors of the post-1945 period made a more conscious effort to shake off some of the recurring characteristics, accepted as the essential pattern of family stories since the earliest moral examples of Maria Edgeworth and Mrs Sherwood.

One of the common conventions of family stories to this day is that of banishing one or both parents. It is possible that this originated from the lower expectation of life of adults before the medical advances of the twentieth century, but this initial reason was perhaps later allied to the idea that greater freedom for children was possible if one or both parents were written out of the story. In *Tales out of school*, Geoffrey Trease maintained that parents were 'perfect, distant or dead', and believed that authors still followed 'the Victorian tradition that a story, whatever else it does, shall not dim the parental halo'. The 1960's showed signs of parental haloes slipping. Joan E Cass pleaded for the inclusion of parents in family stories to lend realism, but stated succinctly the case for parents *in absentia* when she wrote in her book *Literature and the young child* that 'in some stories, even parents harmlessly disappear, and here the unconscious wish of the child to rid himself of those frustrating adults who always prevent him from doing and having everything he wants, finds safe and happy fulfilment'. Thomas Day helped to establish the missing parent tradition in *Sandford and Merton,* a story in which two boys from different backgrounds spent most of their time in the care of their incredibly dull tutor, Mr Barlow. Catherine Sinclair continued the tradition in *Holiday House*: when the mother dies the father goes on a long cruise to recuperate. Nowadays the widower in fact or in fiction would be more likely to be in immediate difficulties over the care of his motherless children, and eventually to remarry, as the widower fathers do in *Selina's new family* by Anne Pilgrim, in *The scapegoat* by Sheena Porter, and in *The battle of Wednesday week* by Barbara Willard. The missing parent tradition is similarly paralleled in America. The father in *Little women,* by Louisa M Alcott, is away during the Civil War; the mother is dead in *What Katy did, by* Susan Coolidge; Ellen Montgomery is sent to live with unsympathetic relations in *The wide, wide world,* by Elizabeth Wetherell; Tom tries to evade his aunt as frequently as possible in *The adventures of Tom Sawyer* by Mark Twain, while Elnora in *A girl of the Limberlost* by Gene Stratton Porter has a difficult time living alone with her warped, widowed mother. The Melendy family of Elizabeth Enright are motherless, and Eleanor Estes' Moffats are fatherless. Mrs E L Konigsburg presented brother and sister efficiently independent in *From the mixed-up files of Mrs Basil E Frankweiler,* but Elizabeth, an only child, is firmly based with both parents in her earlier book: *Jennifer, Hecate, Macbeth and me.* Emily Cheney Neville has shown parents and children occasionally irritating each other almost beyond endurance, but in contrast has also shown a boy having to fend for himself because of his father's lack of interest.

In the European field, parents seem to be even more elusive than elsewhere, but the Commonwealth pattern is more similar to the British and American. Parents seldom departed, even by the 1960's, as a result of divorce. It may be asked whether this is a reflection of attitudes of disapproval, or whether it shows instead an awareness of the delicate and difficult situation which divorce may create for children as well as for adults in real life. In current family stories, it seems that at least forty percent of parents are likely to be missing, the recurring twentieth century hazards for them being death in car or aeroplane crash, or a briefly dismissed 'accident'. Parents die in crashes in *Portrait of Margarita,* by Ruth M Arthur; *The high house,* by Honor Arundel; *Jessica on her own,* by Mary K Harris, and in *The family Tower,* by Barbara Willard. A reviewer of four family stories in the *Times literary supplement,* 3 October 1968, commented that 'sociologists might note the disposal of female parents in the present group of tales'.

The pattern of missing parents is, therefore, common to both earlier and recent family stories, but a more startling contrast between the two lies in the role of the extended family. Nineteenth century families were more closely linked than the majority of present day families, and rallied around each other both in times of trouble and for pleasure to such an extent that there were often minimal links with the outside world, particularly for children. Such close knit family ties are less common today, with the more general dispersal of large family units and greater educational and vocational opportunities available for girls. Boys growing up in the eighteenth or nineteenth century might extend their horizons by going to boarding school, but girls could easily grow up with few connections outside the extended family, apart from the inevitable servants, governess, local doctor or clergyman. There was no question of children choosing their own friends, suitable or otherwise, as there is today. Marghanita Laski pointed out that in only one of the books in her omnibus *Victorian tales for girls* ' do any of the children casually meet and play with other children '. Even with freedom to choose friends, difficulties often arose, as in *The bus girls*, by Mary K Harris; *Pauline*, by Margaret Storey and in *Hell's Edge*, by John Rowe Townsend. Australian friendships showed fewer difficulties arising from class differences in the books of both Eleanor Spence and H F Brinsmead.

It is also noticeable that in earlier family stories, as in real life of the period, children frequently led lives separated from their parents for as many as twenty three hours out of twenty four. Healthy aspects of real life mirrored in family stories of the 1960's were the increased joint activities of parents and children, the relationships between children and other adults, and the friendships considered permissible. *The children of the house*, by Brian Fairfax-Lucy and A Philippa Pearce, set in the early twentieth century, gives a sad picture of four children closely united and feeling more affection for the family servants than for their parents. *The gentle heritage*, by Frances Crompton was a late nineteenth century family story which showed the children amusing themselves independently of their parents, but making friends with a new adult neighbour.

The lives of children in the eighteenth and nineteenth centuries seem grossly circumscribed to children in this more mobile age. Children today would not tolerate some of the petty restrictions imposed by adults in an earlier period. As a result of the greater freedom which children enjoy today, it is conspicuously noticeable how some middle class children in current stories are able to cope with difficult situations beyond the experience of their earlier counterparts: the three children manage admirably in *Castaway Christmas*, by Margaret J Baker; a group of friends face severe testing in *To the wild sky*, by the Australian, Ivan Southall; while peaks of ingenuity enable a brother and sister to carry out their exploit in *From the mixed-up files of Mrs Basil E Frankweiler*, by American Mrs E L Konigsburg. Nineteenth century children, almost wholly dependent on servants, would have been unlikely to manage as well. Nor would all twentieth century children be equal to the strains, as Noel Streatfeild demonstrated in *The growing summer*, in which she dealt with the day to day difficulties of the four Gareth children when, in a family emergency, they were sent to Great-Aunt Dymphna in Ireland, for the summer.

The basic weakness of the family story is that it dates rapidly, which may explain the oblivion into which many family stories eventually sink, although popular in their day. In *Library review*, Summer 1968, the present author wrote in ' To survive or not to survive?' that ' in view of the number of stories of everyday life written annually it is thought provoking to realise the minute proportion that is likely to survive '. It is possible that the family fantasy, less concerned with current social issues, survives better because it is not bound up with contemporary detail. This is certainly true of both Mrs Molesworth and E Nesbit, whose skill with fantasy carries the reader successfully over the occasional out of date passages. With contemporary authors, it seems highly probable that Alan Garner, William Mayne and A Philippa Pearce will still be read when Anne Barrett, Elizabeth Stucley and John Rowe Townsend are forgotten.

chapter two

RELATIONSHIPS INSIDE AND OUTSIDE THE FAMILY

Relationships within the family constitute the essential core of the majority of family stories, although in Britain, in America and throughout the world the family in fiction is frequently incomplete. Each author has to decide whether to give a rounded picture of relationships within a family or to concentrate on a more specific relationship between a parent and child or between a brother and sister. A trend of the 1960's was to deal more frequently with relationships outside the immediate family: those with adults outside the family, and those formed by a child deprived of parents or of siblings. Whichever angle has been chosen has a contribution to make to the young reader's development, by giving at most, a true to life, or at least, a not over romanticised picture of family relationships in addition to a plausible representation of those outside the family. Family stories written with an understanding of the ramifications of family relationships may give a young reader insight into his personal situation: it can be a comfort to realise that it is not abnormal to resent one's parents or to be ashamed of them; to fight with brothers and sisters or to envy them; to yearn for independence.

In the 1960's, stories which attempted to give a realistic picture of family life, with both parents and several children involved, were written by authors who included A Philippa Pearce, William Mayne, Sheena Porter, Jenifer Wayne and Barbara Willard. Family stories from America, by Ruth Forbes Chandler, Emily Cheney Neville and Virginia Sorensen showed both parents and children involved. A closely united family front was emphasised in stories from other countries by P H Nortje, Joan Phipson, Andrew Salkey and Marie Thøger. In *Geoffrey Trease*, a Bodley Head monograph by Margaret Meek, the author commented on the fact that the ' family has ceased to be a group of people bound together by ties of blood and has become the unit of a culture pattern, while the critics seize on the implications of every chintz cover and every tin of beans '.

With or without parents, the emphasis still tended to be on the middle class family in the 1960's, and in the case of Antonia Forest and a few others, upper middle class background was presented. Fathers' careers, as in the Victorian period, tended to be predominantly middle class: in medicine, law, the church, art or literature, although a nominal proportion of fathers in the 1960's carried out the essential jobs of bus, lorry or engine driver, draughtsman, policeman or caretaker. In *Ginger and number 10,* by Prudence Andrew, the fathers of Ginger and the boys in his gang are respectively bricklayer, iron-monger, railwayman and manager of a fish and chip shop. The occupations of the West Indians in the same book include: working in a mortuary, in a slaughter house, in a button factory, weeding a railway track, washing dishes, swabbing lavatories and bathrooms in a mental hospital. Occupations of fathers in America and in other countries tended to be less consistently middle class than those of British fathers: Mr Brown in *Hurricane,* by the Jamaican, Andrew Salkey, is a contractor and builder; Mr Somerville in *The green laurel,* by Australian Eleanor Spence, runs a miniature railway at fairgrounds until incapacitated by ill health; Mr Green in *Beat of the city,* by another Australian, H F Brinsmead, is a housepainter; while Mr Rusch in *Onion John,* by the American, Joseph Krumgold, runs a hardware store. American and Australian family stories of the 1960's also yielded their share of fathers who were lawyers, teachers or businessmen, as is proved in books by Emily Cheney Neville, Mary Stolz, H F Brinsmead, Eleanor Spence and others.

In the 1960's, one or both parents were still banished by death or other means by numerous authors, who included Mary K Harris, Sheena Porter, Margaret Storey, John Rowe Townsend and Philip Turner. This was similar to the pattern of the 1930's when M E Atkinson, Kitty Barne, Arthur Ransome and Noel Streatfeild usually had one, if not both, parents completely out of the story or discreetly in the background. In the 1960's Noel Streatfeild was still skilfully disposing of parents: in *The children on the top floor,* four babies are left on the doorstep of the house of a famous television personality; in *The growing summer,* the father goes abroad to do scientific research, and the mother has to join him when he becomes seriously ill. Although parents, if present in the story, tended to be occasionally more directly involved during the 1960's, there were still family stories which progressed with the minimum of parental assistance. This is true of *Castaway Christmas,* by Margaret J Baker, in which the parents only appear towards the end of the book, after the children have survived on their own for several days, cut off by floods in a remote country house. In *The latchkey children,* by Eric Allen, a group of London children have to manage their own affairs while the mothers go out to work.

When parents are mentioned in a story, they are presented in a variety of ways. Sometimes the reader learns the father's occupation, which may be the author's way of conveying the background of the story, though this may indeed be the most concrete piece of information to be given about the father, apart from his vague presence at family meals, which appear to be one of the most frequently shared family activities: perhaps a reflection of reality. Ideally, fathers emerged as characters in their own rights in books by authors like Margaret J Baker, William Mayne and Sheena Porter, who have all succeeded, with a touch of humour, in presenting fathers with both strengths and weaknesses. The attitudes of these authors to fathers reflect the changes in the role of the father which have occurred during the twentieth century. Two recent books about, rather than for children brought out details of unhappy father and child relationships in the early part of the twentieth century: *The children of the house,* by Brian Fairfax-Lucy and A Philippa Pearce showed a complete lack of communication between two generations; while in *Better to arrive,* by Glenda Gordon, the eight year old Glenda is almost relieved over the death of her forbidding father who, on her birth, refused to see her for months, because the mother had been seriously ill after the birth. Father and child relationships could be unhappy in the 1960's: Maribel Edwin introduced a stern, unsympathetic father in *The snowbound bus,* while in *Midway,* by Anne Barrett, the least brilliant middle member of the family is struggling to gain his distinguished father's approval.

In the 1960's several authors succeeded in presenting fathers with individual personalities in a way not often encountered in earlier family stories. In *The two sisters,* by Honor Arundel, an unusually detailed picture was given of a frustrated, electrician father, whose problems are solved by the end of the book in a manner that seems more possible in fiction than in real life. Mary K Harris created three very different fathers in *The bus girls, Jessica on her own,* and in *Penny's way.* In both *The bus girls* and in *The Paradise summer,* by Priscilla M Warner, details were given of fathers trying to persuade their children to follow careers against the children's own wishes. The father in *Penny's way* is very aware of the value of education, and is bitter because he himself was unable to stay at school to complete his education.

It was a satisfactory feature of some family stories of the 1960's that they reflected adult attitudes, problems and difficulties as well as those of children. Some American writers presented convincingly drawn fathers and clearly illustrated problems of the fathers which sometimes involved the entire family in books like *Miracles on Maple Hill,* by Virginia Sorensen or *Ladder to the sky,* by Ruth Forbes Chandler. In *It's like this, cat,* Emily Cheney Neville pinpointed the strained relationship which can exist between father and son, and showed how it affected the mother. In *Onion John,* by Joseph Krumgold, Andy's father, who runs a hardware store, is another parent eager to inveigle his child into the career he would have liked to follow himself.

Father and son relationships, sketchily glossed over by many authors, were sensitively portrayed by William Mayne in *Earthfasts*, in which the father, a doctor and a widower, is on close terms with his only son; and by Philip Turner in *The Grange at High Force*, which gave three pictures of father and son relationships. The cordial relationship of David, Arthur and Peter with their carpenter, farmer and clergyman fathers are integral links of the story. A less happy father and son relationship was given by K M Peyton in *Fly-by-night*: Peter McNair's strained relationship with his father reaches such an impossible stage that Peter is sent to foster parents for a short period. Mr McNair could be described as a fanatical horse lover, and a similar father, Danny Duncan, was created by Vian Smith in *The Lord Mayor's show*. This is another story which brings out the difficulties which can arise between father and family. Yet another angle on fathers was given by Penelope Farmer in *The magic stone*, in which the father, a writer absorbed in his work, is casual and snappy with his own children, but expands in the presence of another child invited to tea.

Father and daughter relationships were well handled by John Rowe Townsend, Eleanor Spence, Virginia Sorensen and others. In *Hell's Edge*, by John Rowe Townsend, teenager Ril has an almost benevolent attitude towards her absentminded lecturer father, who is yet another widower. A book published in the late 1950's, which must be mentioned here, is *A friend for Frances*, by Priscilla M Warner, which is unusual for its acute handling of both father and daughter and mother and daughter relationships. A good picture of a father and daughter relationship was given in *Miracles on Maple Hill*, by Virginia Sorensen. Ten year old Marly's misery over her father's depression on his return from the second world war is shared by the young reader, who also joins in the family's joy at the father's return to normality. Another satisfactory father and daughter relationship was presented by Eleanor Spence in *The green laurel*, in which the father, forced to spend a long period in hospital, still continues to encourage his shy eldest daughter, Lesley, over a difficult period of adjustment. Acute longing for a father is experienced by twelve year old Loella in *Pappa Pellerin's daughter*, by Swedish Maria Gripe. In the same book, Loella's friend Mona tries to explain to Loella how unsatisfactory her relationship with her father has been and says that 'if Pappa had always been strict and angry and had told her off and shouted at her she would not have minded. If he had forbidden her to smoke or to use make-up or to stay out late it would have been all right. . . . Because that would have meant that he'd have cared about her.'

In most family stories, mothers, if present, tend to play a more prominent part than fathers, perhaps because, as in real life, they are usually more involved with the children, particularly if they are at home and not working elsewhere. In the 1960's, some of the most sympathetic pictures of mothers were drawn by Mary K Harris, Jenifer Wayne and Barbara Willard. Gone forever are the elegant, delicate mothers of the Victorian era, who alternated between languishing on their chaises longues and attending to the intricacies of visiting cards. In favour of today's less leisurely atmosphere is the fact that in fiction, as in real life, most parents are involved in their children's lives to an extent not even imagined possible forty years ago. The reader of today is appalled at the casual attitudes of comfortably off middle class parents in the 1930's, reflected in a book like *Alice, Thomas, and Jane* by Enid Bagnold, in which the mother, attired in her swimsuit, is more concerned over her day's programme on the beach, and over preserving peace with the cook, than about the activities of her three children, in the care of a governess who frequently leaves them to their own devices.

This mother of the 1930's makes a glaring contrast to Mrs Grey, the small, insignificant widow in *The bus girls* by Mary K Harris, who struggles to make ends meet in a later period, by sewing curtains and chair covers, and denies herself food and clothing to give her delicate daughter Hetty a good education. Hetty, absorbed in a rewarding school life, is bored and irritated by her mother and ashamed of her feelings. The mother in *Private beach,* by Richard Parker, is attuned to her family of five, each with his or her peculiar foible. Anne Pilgrim gave a convincing picture of mother and daughter difficulties in *Selina's new family,* while in *Clemence and Ginger,* Jenifer Wayne described with insight the difficulties of a mother who tries to combine running the house with writing. Less congenial mothers were created by Anne Barrett, Annabel Farjeon, Sheena Porter and John Rowe Townsend. In *Nordy Bank,* Sheena

Porter humorously brought out the conflicting attitudes both of a casual mother and of an over fussy mother on such topics as children, houses and dogs. In both *Hell's Edge* and *Pirate's island,* John Rowe Townsend depicted mothers blunderingly mishandling their offspring because they are unable to perceive their children's particular needs. Annabel Farjeon gave an unattractive picture of a nagging, discontented mother in *Maria Lupin.* In children's books, American mothers appear to have an image different from their British counterparts. The reader gains impressions of over-anxious American mothers, of mothers more eager to be independent of their offspring than the average British mother, and of mothers pushing their children's social development in ways that might not even occur to their British counterparts. Such impressions are gained from books by Ruth Forbes Chandler, Mrs E L Konigsburg and Emily Cheney Neville.

Mothers from Australia emerged as particularly hardworking in books like *The family conspiracy* by Joan Phipson, or *The green laurel* by Eleanor Spence but, in contrast, a most searching picture of a feather-brained mother was given by Ivan Southall in *To the wild sky,* in which Mrs Bancroft was described with heartless detail as jealous of her daughter and of what her daughter might become, but she loved her in a frightened way just the same. Later in the same book, at the height of a crisis which involves several children as the result of an aeroplane crash, Mrs Bancroft's daughter Carol thinks ' How would her mother behave? She'd be hysterical, probably; inconsolable, probably. A woman without backbone, that was her mother: a small, fluffy, silly, slightly brassy sort of woman, running to fat, whose world was fashion magazines and hair styles and diet plans and a blind conviction that she was beautiful. But she had a heart for all that; there were many mothers less motherly.'

It proves easier to find examples of mother and daughter relationships than mother and son relationships. A factor contributing to this may be that family stories are mainly written for girls, but this theory does not explain the reason for the higher incidence of father and son relationships. Different pictures of mother and daughter relationships were successfully drawn in the 1960's by Mary K Harris, Richard Parker, Anne Pilgrim and Mary Treadgold. In *Penny's way,* Mary K Harris showed a harassed mother finding difficulty in keeping pace with her three teenage daughters. Selina, in *Selina's new family,* by Anne Pilgrim, is over-dependent on her widowed mother, and suffers cataclysmic reactions when her mother remarries. In *Private beach*, by Richard Parker, the mother treats the eldest daughter, Alice, like a grown-up, and appeals to her for help in handling family frictions. The widowed mother in *The winter princess*, by Mary Treadgold, has good relationships with her daughters Sarah and Marilla. The 1960's could not produce a book to equate with *A friend for Frances*, by Priscilla M Warner, with its painfully realistic picture of strained mother and daughter relationships. Family stories give an impression that closer relationships exist between widows and widowers and their offspring than between other parents and their children.

Details of bad or good mother and son relationships are few and far between. In *Songberd's Grove*, by Anne Barrett, the only son Martin shows concern over his mother, while Bill, in *No boats on Bannermere*, by Geoffrey Trease, commends his mother for being a credit to him and for knowing how to behave to please a growing son; attitudes which strike the reader as condescending. Both these examples are pre-1960. *Pirate's island*, by John Rowe Townsend, written in the 1960's, but dealing with an earlier period, gave a good picture of Gordon's mother: bossy, pompous, over-protective and completely unable to manage her fat, timorous and not very bright son. In *The pavilion*, by Elfrida Vipont, Martin looks ruefully at his mother, who is a writer, and wishes that she took a little more interest in her appearance. With the perceptiveness of youth, he wonders if she had long ago given up any hope of competing with her glamorous actress sister, Milly.

Relationships between parents and children have been briefly considered, but an important part of any successful family story is the picture that it gives of relationships between the children of the family: between brothers, between sisters or between brothers and sisters. Relations between siblings can be amicable, competitive, over-dependent, jealous or of many other degrees of depth. Often brother and sister relationships are an incidental but essential part of the story, as in books by Mary K Harris, William Mayne, Sheena Porter or Barbara Willard, who, in the 1960's, all gave convincing details both of the camaraderie and of the running warfare which constitute family relationships.

28

In other stories, sibling relationships formed a main or secondary theme, and an attempt was made to throw a searchlight on some of the sharp conflicts which occurred. The relationship between two brothers was an important part of *The plan for Birdsmarsh* by K M Peyton, of whom John Rowe Townsend wrote in the *Wilson library bulletin*, October 1968, that ' though she has a strong feeling for time and place, her true concern is always for people, their individual complexities and their relationships '. The acute feelings of inferiority of Mark, who compares himself unfavourably with his clever brothers and sister, were skilfully portrayed by Anne Barrett in *Midway*. The ambivalent feelings of Ben towards grown-up sisters absorbed in planning one sister's wedding, and towards younger brothers absorbed in trivia, were captured by A Philippa Pearce in *A dog so small*. In *Penny's way*, by Mary K Harris, the relationships of a family of three sisters were portrayed with special emphasis on the role of the youngest sister, Penny, while in *Jessica on her own*, her last book written before she died, Mary K Harris presented another family of three entirely different sisters from the angle of the middle sister, Jessica, who attends a secondary modern school, while her clever and loquacious elder sister goes to a grammar school and her spoiled, precocious younger sister attends a private school. Rich sister relationships and brother and sister relationships were challengingly covered by Antonia Forest in her books about the Marlow family. In the 1960's other parts of the world yielded realistic details of brother and sister relationships in such books as *Hurricane*, by Andrew Salkey; *Patterson's Track*, by Eleanor Spence and *Ladder to the sky*, by Ruth Forbes Chandler.

The striking fact is that there is not a wider range of family stories set in the 1960's which present relationships between siblings. These relationships may have regularly been handled with little or no depth for two reasons: in real life family ties have come to mean less than formerly, and authors may also have found it extremely difficult to give convincing details of the relationships of a generation younger than their own. It is perhaps easier to find outstanding examples of personal relationships in types of children's books other than the family story—a severe condemnation of the family story. Historical novels, written in the 1960's, were rich in details of good, bad, conflicting and involved relationships: Leon Garfield, K M Peyton, Barbara Leonie Picard and Rosemary Sutcliff all provided examples of relationships within or beyond the family, often treated with far more depth than in books classified as family stories.

The interminable difficulties that relationships can cause in real life may partially account for the recurring source of fascination which only children provide in fiction. The disgruntled may dream of a more idyllic existence unencumbered by siblings. On neither side of the Atlantic can family stories be accused of pandering to this type of wish fulfilment, as in most cases in fiction the only child's lot does not prove to be an enviable one: Ruth M Arthur, Sheena Porter, John Rowe Townsend, Philip Turner and Barbara Willard all proved this in the 1960's, while in America Mrs E L Konigsburg, Joseph Krumgold and Emily Cheney Neville all dealt with some of the difficulties. In *Beat of the city*, Australian H F Brinsmead gave an uncomfortable picture of an only son, spoiled in childhood, who grows up to despise and ridicule his hard working parents, while in her book, *Pastures of the blue crane*, H F Brinsmead proved that the lot of an orphaned only daughter, even if free of financial difficulties, is not an easy one. Ril, in *Hell's Edge*, by John Rowe Townsend, has to adjust to a new industrial environment, when her father moves from a quiet seaside town to a new lecturing post. She feels adultly responsible for her absentminded father, and in *The Hallersage sound*, the sequel to *Hell's Edge*, has to face new difficulties when her father marries her headmistress. Margarita, whose parents are killed in an air crash at the start of *Portrait of Margarita*, by Ruth M Arthur, has to face up to acceptance of her parents' deaths, recognition of her unexpected feelings for her retiring guardian, and assimilation into a new community. The only daughter who loses both parents was a recurring theme in the 1960's, successfully tackled by Mary K Harris in *Seraphina*, by Margaret Storey in *Pauline* and by Barbara Willard in *Charity at home*. In *Deerfold* by Sheena Porter, Megan, who has accepted her life in Radnor without question until her teens, is filled with new doubts and criticisms when a town family come to live nearby. Nevertheless, some children may imagine that the supposed calm of an only child's life is preferable to the hurly burly of modern family life in a small house in which the mother manages with no domestic help and perhaps holds down an outside job as well.

If only children provide wish fulfilment in family stories, twins are an almost equally fascinating source of wish fulfilment. Geoffrey Trease pointed out in *Tales out of school* that there seem to be far more twins in fiction than in real life. The attractions may include the idea of a brother and sister of exactly the same age, and of similar if not identical appearance, the joint sharing of all activities both at school and at home, and the comic possibilities of identical twins. In the 1930's twins abounded in the works of Kitty Barne, Eva Garnett, Eleanor Graham and Arthur Ransome, but in the 1960's they were harder to trace: Adam and Lucy were the clever twins in *Midway* by Anne Barrett; since 1948 Antonia Forest's twins, Nicky and Laurie, have gradually grown up in her series of school and family stories about the Marlow family; while Barbara Willard introduces not only one set of twins but two, in *The family Tower* and its sequel *The toppling Towers*.

Family stories in the 1960's frequently failed to give a balanced picture of family relationships, but this fault is even more true of stories of the 1930's and 1940's. If details of nuclear family life in the 1960's are sketchy, the reader hesitates to consider how extended family relationships are handled; occasionally more sympathetically and in more detail than immediate family relationships, but it may be a reflection of real life that extended family relationships tend to be of decreasing importance, although this is not always true. *Wild goose summer,* by South African P H Nortje may have expressed widely unacceptable attitudes to the coloured boys on the farm, but showed strong solidarity within both the immediate and the extended family. The critic would have difficulty in producing a British book in which ' Dad began paging through Bible in search of a reading for the day ', while ' Mum said a short prayer in a hushed but steady voice, and asked that each one of us should be guided by His eternal wisdom. Her heart was full of gratitude because there was peace and happiness and love in our house.' In *A dog so small,* A Philippa Pearce gave a most thorough and carefully detailed picture of Ben's grandparents: the grandmother forceful and domineering and the grandfather retiring and gentle, frightened to offer his own opinions. Ben's grandparents, and those created by Josephine Kamm in *No strangers here*, and by Elizabeth Stucley in *Magnolia Buildings*, all demonstrated the unchanging life of older people who had stayed in the country while the next generation moved to the city. The grandmother played an essential part in *The boy who wasn't lonely*, by Richard Parker, in which the only child, Cricket, prefers to visit his grandmother rather than his young cousins; but a very unsympathetic picture of grandparents was given in *Jennifer, Hecate, Macbeth and me*, by Mrs E L Konigsburg. From Italy came a most moving picture of the very close relationship between a boy and his grandmother in *Za the truffle boy*, by Angela Latini, who wrote that 'I intended this story to be about Za. But Za's grandmother was everything to him, and how can one talk about a boy and be silent about the chief person in his world? So it is about them both. It has to be.' Both grandmothers play important roles in *Shanta*, by Marie Thøger. The grandmother of Antonia Forest's Marlows is a dragon-like figure, who worships her grandsons but has no time for her granddaughters.

It is easier to find vivid details of relationships between grandmothers and grandchildren than to find situations which involve the grandfathers. *A dog so small*, by A Phillipa Pearce, is one of the few books in which both grandparents play essential parts. *Pastures of the blue crane*, by H F Brinsmead, is unusual with its convincing account of the adjustment of Ryl and her unknown grandfather, when they are thrown together on the death of her father. In *The cloud with the silver lining*, the Jamaican writer, C Everard Palmer, gave an account of the commendable efforts of Timmy and his elder brother Milton to raise funds to buy a buggy for their grandfather, who at the opening of the story has to have a leg amputated after his donkey has thrown him. A sympathetic picture of a relationship between grandfather and grandson, closer than that between father and son, was given by Aidan Chambers in *Marle*.

Some family stories of the 1960's gave the impression that relations, apart from parents and perhaps grandparents, were only an undesirable necessity after the death of parents. Mary K Harris clearly described the conflicting outlooks of her eponymous orphan Seraphina and her maiden aunt, a successful hairdresser who expects Seraphina to join her in the business rather than to follow the career of her own choice. In *The high house*, Honor Arundel wrote of a brother and sister orphaned as a result of a motor crash, who are sent to live with two sisters of completely different dispositions. There are startling contrasts in the two sisters' modes of life. Emma goes to the somewhat Bohemian aunt in Edinburgh, while Richard, whose new life is touched on more briefly, goes to the over-fussy, colourless aunt whose worst offence, in Richard's eyes, is her production of the same menus every week. Barbara Willard sympathetically showed the difficulties of both the orphan Charity and the aunt who becomes her guardian. A slightly sad picture of a boy's relationship with his aunt and uncle was given in *A Severnside story*, by Frederick Grice, in which Jimmy Tansell is brought up by his uncle and aunt, Mr and Mrs Fearis, because his father has been killed in the war, and his mother has died shortly after running away with another man.

If the parents were not killed off in accidents in the family stories of the 1960's, there were often other situations or emergencies which demanded the presence of relatives, to stand *in loco parentis*. An aunt such as Cousin Paula in *The hunt for Harry*, by Rosemary Weir, is nowadays as unlikely in real life as in fiction. Great-Aunt Dymphna in *The growing summer* by Noel Streatfeild, is a true character, preserving her own sometimes trying individuality in a period when conformity is the norm. Aunt Borage, in *Cut off from crumpets* by Margaret J Baker, is another larger than life personality, who specialises in odd presents from bazaars, drives an ex-mail van, is more concerned over her dogs' welfare than over her own, and sums up her situation as ' I've no family of my own and all the time in the world '.

Relationships within the family were sometimes less adequately treated in family stories of the 1960's than relationships outside the family. The 1960's showed a tendency for authors to give more rounded pictures than many of their predecessors of relationships between children and adults outside the family. It seems a desirable feature of family stories to portray good relations between different generations, and in the 1960's this was successfully achieved by Ruth M Arthur, Honor Arundel, William Mayne, John Rowe Townsend, Philip Turner and Barbara Willard. In *Requiem for a princess*, Ruth M Arthur showed how a sympathetic adult helps a teenager over a very difficult period of adjustment, when rent by the traumatic experience of discovering that she is adopted. The families from different backgrounds, in *Green Street* by Honor Arundel, have healthy relationships with adults involved in art, local government, law and trade. William Mayne and Philip Turner created adults in their books such as Miss Durnthwaite or the Admiral, with human failings and idiosyncrasies which the children accept. John Rowe Townsend and Barbara Willard showed grown-ups outside the family playing an important part in children's development. In *Pirate's island,* by John Rowe Townsend, a sympathetic clergyman and his wife help to rehabilitate Sheila, a child from a very poor family. Mr Tressider plays a different part in *Charity at home,* by Barbara Willard: he arouses Charity's interest in beautiful things and encourages her latent artistic ability. In some children's books of the 1960's, adults outside the family were sometimes more involved with the children than their shadowy parents. This was true of *The adventures of five children and a dog,* by Italian Renée Reggiani, in which Turi, a musical young workman, forms a children's band, and is followed to Milan by the children when he wins a bandmaster scholarship. In spite of the children leaving their own families to be with Turi, one of the boys, Pickles, realises that 'family ties and adventures often lead in two opposite directions', but 'a desire for adventure does not put an end to family ties; funnily enough it sometimes strengthens them '.

Relationships within the immediate and extended family, and with adults outside the family, have been briefly considered, but an important part of any family story is its treatment of the relationships between children. Authors handle these relationships with varying degrees of success. In the eighteenth and nineteenth centuries, children were not free to choose their friends as they were by the 1960's. The two situations have been clearly reflected in earlier children's books as against those published in the 1960's.

Freedom of choice presents its own problems. Sheena Porter, Margaret Storey and Honor Arundel all attempted to deal with possible difficulties. In *Deerfold* by Sheena Porter, Megan makes new friends from a town, and leads them to believe that she comes from a more prosperous background than is in fact the case. Margaret Storey's *Pauline* illustrated the difficulties which can arise when adults disapprove of young people's friendships. Mary K Harris was adept at showing the problems of unattractive and uncongenial girls desperately eager to be friendly with other girls who do not reciprocate their feelings. This author also gave a vivid and sensitive account of Seraphina's friendship with Stephanie.

Friendship was handled with more depth than is usually found, in *The magic stone* by Penelope Farmer, which is a satisfactory blend of realism and fantasy. This is another example of a friendship between two girls from different backgrounds, but in spite of difficulties and quarrels, Caroline eventually realises that ' she had always assumed that friendship was words and talking, like the pairs of best friends who whispered in corners at school, who giggled and told secrets and shut you out, looking to see that you could not hear, giggling at you. . . . And now with Alice it seemed to her that the great test of being friends was not talk but silence, knowing how to be silent with someone, not needing to talk to keep a weak friendship alive.' Boys' friendships have been skilfully presented by E W Hildick, William Mayne and Philip Turner. In the 1950's, E W Hildick made a new contribution to the story of everyday life with the creation of Jim Starling and his friends at Cement Street Secondary Modern School. In the 1960's he dealt with another neglected area in *The questers*, in which Peter's friends rally round to entertain him when he is confined to bed for a long period. This book has technical weaknesses, but deserves mention for its treatment of friendship maintained under difficulties. William Mayne and Philip Turner gave more normal pictures of schoolboy friendships, with their fierce though transitory enthusiasms, in books like *Sand*, or *The Grange at High Force*.

In the 1960's, various patterns in the presentation of relationships emerged. Parents, if present at all, were often more involved in the story than their counterparts in the stories of everyday life written in the 1930's. J K G Taylor believed that by the 1950's ' parents are revealed as people rather than symbols. They enter more into the activities of the children, sometimes share the same fears and anxieties, sometimes discuss problems of a real kind '. It appears to be easier to find examples of father and daughter, mother and daughter, father and son relationships than to find examples of mother and son relationships. Any theory that mother and son relationships may be of less interest in a class of book generally aimed mainly at girls is disproved by the number of books which give details of father and son relationships. Though mother and son relationships are widely believed to have adverse psychiatric possibilities.

Relationships within the extended family occurred less frequently in the 1960's than in the 1930's and earlier. Nowadays the extended family appears to be of use mainly when parents have died, so that unfortunate aunts, uncles and cousins have to take charge of equally unfortunate orphans. Perhaps the best examples of extended family relationships were those with grandparents, which in a few cases were handled more fully than relations with parents. This may support the theory that there can be more *rapport* between grandchildren and grandparents than is possible between children and parents.

A conspicuous feature of family stories in the 1960's was the more detailed presentation of adults, both within and without the family, which in turn caused fuller treatment of their relationships with children. It is sometimes revealing in family stories of the 1960's to be given a clear picture of not only children's problems, but also of those of adults.

In the 1960's there was a dearth of outstanding examples of relationships between members of the same generation. An adult writer may have found difficulty in giving a true and convincing picture of the present-day relationships of a younger generation, but it is a trenchant condemnation of family stories of the last decade, that, in spite of authors frequently presenting adequate pictures of relationships between children and adults, they neglect in numerous instances to present with any depth the relationships between young people. In the 1960's the increasing amount of material from America, from the Commonwealth and available in translation in Britain, helped by its treatment of relationships between young people in other countries, to extend the horizons of British children growing up in an increasingly mobile society.

36

EVERYDAY LIFE OF THE 1960's REFLECTED IN
THE FAMILY STORY

The casual reader of children's books might easily gain the impressions that the representation of normal daily life in them is nominal, and that fictional life is a series of mysteries, adventures and holidays, preferably with little or no adult supervision. These impressions would be less valid for the 1960's than for the 1930's, when the cult of the holiday adventure story perhaps reached its peak, but nevertheless Margery Fisher wrote in *Intent upon reading* that ' family stories are often as unreal as the most far-fetched yarn . . . Children are left on their own quite as much as they are in stories of gangsters and smugglers. Their parents are barely glimpsed in the background '. By the 1960's, writers were very gradually realising that stories based on everyday life could provide experiences, problems and conflicts more absorbing than any encountered in stories of repetitive treasure hunts or of superficial mysteries. As Terry's mother said to her in *The year of the currawong*, by Australian Eleanor Spence, ' told the right way, even ordinary little everyday things can be interesting. But you don't have to stick absolutely to facts. You can't make your appletree bear blossoms in July, but you can give

37

it in September much bigger and better blossoms than it might actually have '.

It is obviously not desirable to clamp down on the imaginative talents of an author, but it does seem desirable for authors to combine imagination with realistic background, a feat achieved by a select few, who include Alan Garner, William Mayne and A Philippa Pearce. Authors who lacked great imaginative skill, but who were capable of portraying down to earth real life, rather than some make believe existence which had the sole purpose of providing wish fulfilment, made a useful contribution to the family story in the 1960's. Unfortunately some writers tended to become too moralistic and instructive, a phenomenon described by Claire Tomalin in *The observer,* December 8 1968, as ' the faintly prevailing didactic tone '. Over at least two centuries, a pendulum has swung between entertainment and instruction in children's books. It will be regrettable if the 1960's is remembered as the decade when the pendulum swung too sharply towards instruction. Ideally, writers of children's books should present a recognisable picture of everyday life which stops short of being a sociological document, but all too few give adequate detail of reality. In *Ash Road,* by the Australian, Ivan Southall, three boys are allowed to camp on their own after permission has been reluctantly extracted from their parents. Ivan Southall wrote that ' they wanted none of the trappings of the adult world. They wanted freedom from home, from reminders of school or study, from the endless round of errand-running, music practice, sisters, lawn-mowing and hot showers. No dressing up for visitors or for Sunday. No shoe-cleaning or rigorous tooth-brushing after each meal. No going to bed while still wide awake. No getting up while still half asleep '. In this short passage Ivan Southall has admirably captured the humdrum monotony of the boys' daily lives.

A statement much criticised when first made in the 1930's, and equally open to criticism today, is Paul Hazard's dictum from *Books, children and men,* that ' England could be entirely reconstructed from its children's books '. This theory could hardly be applied successfully to English children's books of the 1930's, which, in spite of widespread unemployment, economic difficulties and international unrest at the time, continued to give the impression of solid, leisurely upper middle class life continuing regardless of external circumstances. In 1952 Frank Eyre wrote in *Twentieth century children's books* that there was ' no sign, as yet, of the development of any type of story dealing with the background and interests of the great majority of the new junior reading public that compulsory education has brought into being '.

By the late 1950's the scene in children's stories of everyday life was slowly spreading to more proletarian ground; this trend continued in the 1960's, but it is still questionable whether the overall picture gained from family stories of the 1960's is representative enough to fulfil Paul Hazard's theory much more successfully than in the 1930's. It is also highly suspect whether children necessarily want to read about backgrounds or about activities in home and school which are too similar to their own. Books are an essential means of extending horizons.

By the end of the 1960's there were indications of this elementary fact being overlooked. Material in contemporary books and in periodical articles often reaches hysterical proportions on, for example, the current social bogey of ' class ', as reflected in children's literature. In *Intent upon reading*, Margery Fisher expressed the (probably accurate) theory that children are likely to be more sane about the class issue than adults. A variety of books in the 1960's, by Honor Arundel, Mary K Harris, Sheena Porter and others showed how children bridged class barriers, not always without difficulties. Margaret Meek thought that class differences were more or less imaginary, and was horrified to discover her error. In *Geoffrey Trease*, her monograph for Bodley Head, she wrote: ' I once believed that the subtle imaginative process of identification enabled children to leap all barriers between their lives and those of the heroes, but classroom experience taught me that it is easier to make contact with the feudal aristocracy than with children who have expensive holidays '. In *Tales out of school*, Geoffrey Trease, himself aware of the pitfalls facing authors who become too class conscious, hoped that they ' will not fall into the error of supposing that the reader from the tenement or the council house is interested only in seeing the realities of his own life reflected '.

At the end of the 1960's this danger was epitomised in the production of Leila Berg's 'Nipper' books, expressly for working class
children, and often the shiftless working class at that. During the
1960's there were more examples published of stories of working
class life than in the preceding decades, but a significant point about
the family stories published in the 1960's is that it is easier to
reconstruct from them the affluent middle class life or the penurious
working class life, than ways of life falling between the two extremes,
partially reflected in books like *Elidor* by Alan Garner, *Fly-by-night*
by K M Peyton, *A parcel of trees* by William Mayne, or *Clemence
and Ginger* by Jenifer Wayne.

A worthwhile line of enquiry is to select a variety of topics common in everyday life with the purpose of considering how they were
covered in family stories of the 1960's. They might include home
life, holidays, outings, special occasions, school life, interests, hobbies
and sports, pets. A short survey of such aspects of everyday life
cannot hope to be exhaustive, but it may help to give some idea of
the image of the 1960's which was presented to the readers. It is
necessary to remember that the child who reads only a few books is
in danger of gaining a distorted view of reality, a fact well illustrated
by Rosemary Weir's *The real game*. In this book, a brother and sister
growing up in Australia base their picture of life in England in the
1960's on *Little Lord Fauntleroy*, by Mrs Frances Hodgson Burnett,
originally published in 1886. It is alarming to wonder how many
equally false impressions real children gain from their reading: a
book like *The Scotch twins*, by Lucy Fitch Perkins, originally published in 1922, is still in print and on some public library shelves,
yet it gives a picture of Scottish life which bears little or no resem-
blance to the life of the majority of Scottish children in the 1960's.
With the rising interchange of children's books between different
countries, it is of more importance than ever before for authors to
represent accurately the life in their particular countries, but to avoid
the error of becoming too didactic.

The accounts given by authors of home life in the 1960's were
frequently more detailed than was the custom in the 1930's, when
normal home life was usually a neglected topic, and was more diverse

than in the nineteenth century portrayals of a secure, middle class background. By the 1960's one of the most common family meetings in the home is seen to be at meal times, a situation apparently prevalent in all parts of the world. The later sociologist, studying children's books for details of life in the 1960's might draw a blank regarding some aspects of the life of the period, but could certainly obtain reasonable, if not always strictly accurate, details of feeding habits, not only in Britain, but also in other parts of the world. *In-between Miya,* by Yoshiko Uchida, gives readers outside Japan a mouth-watering desire for such delicacies as yellow pickled radish, egg custard with bamboo shoots, meat balls with slices of ginger root, rice sprinkled with sesame seed and other national dishes. It is questionable whether the Japanese reader of British children's books would be equally eager to sample our indeterminate 'cold meat', fish and chips, kippers, sausages, baked beans, sandwich pastes and cornflakes, all of which are mentioned with monotonous regularity by British authors. A foreign reader could be forgiven for dismissing British food as stodgy, dull, repetitive and unimaginative.

It is a relief to find the occasional book with interesting descriptions of British meals. A typically British meal in the North country is 'high tea', described at a supreme peak by Philip Turner in *Colonel Sheperton's clock.* He wrote that 'the meal started with two boiled eggs apiece, home-cured ham and sausages. There was an apple-pie to follow, and a fruit cake, and a new white loaf with a full pound of Wensleydale cheese and a pot of honey, and scones and a plate of Darley oatcakes. To wash it all down, there was tea drunk out of mugs which held nearly a pint'. It has to be accepted however, that the baked beans or bacon and egg menus are more true to life in most cases than those with chicken and almonds, peach flan, apple snow and cream or 'a dish of rice, prawns and mushrooms and green peppers'. Class distinctions are no less noticeable with food than with other social habits and customs. Some basic British menus may be classless: roast meat and vegetables followed by fruit pies and the ubiquitous custard; but delicacies such as caviar, *sorbet,* olives or 'gentleman's relish', are all clear indications of the locations of particular stories.

Another peculiarly British institution, afternoon tea, has been mentioned by such different writers as Antonia Forest, Geoffrey Trease and Elfrida Vipont since the 1950's, so that readers outside Britain should by now have a fairly accurate knowledge of old silver, lace tablecloths, delicate china, cucumber sandwiches, China tea and similar joys. The custom of afternoon tea may account for the British interest in every sort of cake and pastry. In addition to the fruit cakes, chocolate cakes, gooseberry, blackberry or apple pies referred to in various books, an interesting list of cakes to be baked for a school sale was given in *The bus girls*, by Mary K Harris. They include cornflake cookies, jam tarts, éclairs, meringues, gingerbreads, Dundee cakes.

Another British dish is the ' sweet ', or common pudding. Although exotic sweets mentioned in family stories of the 1960's included chocolate mousse, peach melba, and lemon meringue pie, the most frequently mentioned pudding appears to have been the homely treacle variety! There is a depreciatory reference to a badly made semolina pudding in Sheena Porter's *Deerfold*. The British may hang their heads in shame over the pedestrian nature of their cooking which is reflected in the majority of children's books, yet it is debatable whether the many international dishes mentioned in British children's stories of the 1960's are necessarily commendable: *poulet* sauté, red-pepper stews, Chicken Maryland, chop suey, sweet and sour pork, veal and noodles, Spanish omelet.

If authors in the 1960's were not presenting family meals, they may have been writing about children helping at home, breakfasting in bed, gardening, playing games, caring for pets, squabbling with siblings, or just being children. Willam Mayne, Sheena Porter and Barbara Willard all excel in the presentation of daily *minutiae*, which can only be done by perceptive observers of reality. One of the richest descriptions of the start of an ordinary day can be found in *Summer visitors*, by William Mayne, which gives all the complex details of the Taylor family's morning programme: the order of rising, the various rituals and, finally, the dressing of the little sister Betty. In Sheena Porter's *Hills and hollows*, there are details of a typical family evening during which the various members of the family are engaged with fish, mice, dominoes, knitting, the local newspaper, poetry and arithmetic. On a Sunday morning members of the same family are occupied with different tasks: peeling potatoes, picking daffodils and cleaning a bicycle. *A parcel of trees,* by William Mayne bristles with details of normal everyday life: helping father in the village home bakery, washing dishes, shopping, delivering messages, titivating for an outing, rooting among junk in the loft, dividing a shared bedroom with tape. The parents in *Meet Lemon Kelly,* by E W Hildick, spend the evening sitting in front of television: father with brown ale and his pipe, and mother with milk stout and darning. *Katrin,* by Swedish Nan Inger gives good everyday details of such activities as exercising the dog, putting the baby to bed, and pushing the family out to school and work in the morning. Before 1960 Eleanor Estes lovingly recounted the timeless details of everyday life in *The Moffats,* which opens with Jane marvelling at the speed and artistry with which her mother peels apples.

It is possible to provide too much sociological detail in family stories, as well as to neglect it, as was the tendency in the 1930's. From the 1950's there were signs of an increasing sense of sociological purpose on the part of writers for children, typified in a book like *A pair of Jesus-boots,* by Sylvia Sherry, which provides a mine of information for the sociologist. The author's vividly detailed descriptions remain firmly in the mind's eye; it is hardly possible to forget descriptions like that of the drab living room in Rocky O'Rourke's home, of which Sylvia Sherry wrote that ' the small electric fire gave off little heat, and neither Rocky nor Suzie took off their outdoor clothes. The only new object in the room was the television set. A mat, dirtied to a dull grey, lay before the hearth, the rest of the floor was covered in linoleum. The faded curtains drooped at the window, a sagging sofa was pushed against one wall, a bed which Suzie and Mrs Flanagan shared against another. A gas-stove and a sink had been fitted into a dark corner. It was a cheerless, dirty room . . .' This book is set in Liverpool, with references to the cathedrals, to the pier head, to Princes Park and other recognisable landmarks.

In the 1960's, authors more frequently used the successful device of a clearly recognisable location for stories of everyday life. London was the setting for stories by several authors, including Eric Allen,

43

Prudence Andrew, A Philippa Pearce and Mary Treadgold. Shropshire was chosen by Sheena Porter for some of her stories, while Yorkshire was the setting for books by both William Mayne and Philip Turner. Alan Garner has written brilliant fantasy, with *Elidor* opening in Manchester, then moving to Cheshire, and *The owl service* set in Wales. In the 1960's, Honor Arundel made Edinburgh come alive for young readers, and in complete contrast, chose an island near Oban for the setting of *Emma's island*.

From family stories of the 1960's, readers both in Britain and abroad can gain a fairly general picture of Britain, provided that they read a wide enough selection of books. An interesting overall impression is that, in fiction if not in fact, there is still a pull towards the country, and some stories attempt to show the respective advantages and disadvantages of both town and country life. Of a sample one hundred British books published in the 1960's, fifty four percent were set in the country, twenty five percent in small towns and the remaining twenty one percent in cities. The small proportion of stories set in cities is surprising in view of the increase in conurbations. Authors may have chosen rural settings as more congenial than urban environments, and may also have considered that rural settings had more to offer for plots than towns or cities. Perhaps the 1960's will be remembered in part as a nostalgic decade, when authors tried to convey the essence of country life before the cities encroached still further on the lives of the majority.

The 1960's deserve to be remembered as a period, when, as never before, it was first possible for young readers to gain vivid, usually fairly accurate pictures of the lives of children in many other parts of the world: the United States, Australia, Ghana, Nigeria, India, Jamaica, Japan, South Africa and various countries in Europe. This increased availability of material from abroad not only brought sometimes startling contrasts in ways of life, and in the nature of problems, but also emphasised quite definitely the universal pattern of many family relationships, and of at least some family problems, whatever the divergences of other ways of life. The differences are starkly noticeable in a book like *Shanta*, by Marie Thøger, set in India, which shows a basically different way of life and a family pattern alien to the British. American author Emily Cheney Neville and Australians H F Brinsmead and Ivan Southall are all adept at bringing out the particular characteristics of their countries, while at the same time emphasising the universality of personal relationships and of personal problems.

Apart from the recurring daily activities which throw the members of a family together are the more special family occasions such as Christmas, birthdays, holidays, and family outings to visit friends or relatives, or to go to cinema, concert, exhibition, theatre, museum, zoo, park or other place of interest. Christmas is probably the most frequently mentioned family occasion in stories of everyday life from all parts of the world. This makes it possible for children to learn how Christmas customs vary in different countries. Many of Howard Spring's convincing details of an English Christmas in *Tumbledown Dick,* originally published in 1939, could still be used to describe the occasion in the 1960's. He wrote of the Christmas dinner, which consisted of turkey, baked potatoes, Brussels sprouts and Christmas pudding. A similar picture was given in *Eileen of Redstone Farm,* in which Alice Lunt described the children's preparations for Christmas, as well as Christmas day itself. The importance of the preparations was also stressed in *Charity at home,* by Barbara Willard, which along with *Jennifer, Hecate, Macbeth and me* by Mrs E L Konigsburg, recorded the feelings, sometimes of disappointment, that can be experienced. Mrs Konigsburg was almost brutal in her descriptions of the grandparents' arrival for Christmas with their own supplies of vegetarian food, their habit of echoing each other's conversation, their over-zealous babysitting, while in the background the mother is constantly running around the house with her vacuum cleaner to remove traces of the vegetarian food.

The essential spirit of Christmas is best captured by writers like Elfrida Vipont, some of whose books are pre-1960, and American Ruth Forbes Chandler. Maria Gripe and Nan Inger have both written of some of the Swedish Christmas customs, while C Everard Palmer and Eleanor Spence have dealt with Jamaican and Australian variations respectively. An unusual British Christmas was described in *Castaway Christmas,* by Margaret J Baker, which offered a sharp contrast to the more traditional family event mentioned in *Guide dog,* by Dorothy Clewes, in which Roley Rolandson considers his family's

Christmas, and recognises the humour of the situation when he thinks that ' two lots of aunts and uncles and five cousins were coming to stay, the place would be bursting at the seams but it was something that happened every year and wouldn't be Christmas without them all being together. When it was over Roley's father always said— Never again—but was first with plans when next year came round '.

Like Christmas, a birthday can cause a child either jubilation, or in some cases, acute frustration. In fiction the reader can find various examples of the latter. In *A dog so small*, by A Philippa Pearce, he shares the bitter disappointment of Ben when he receives a tapestry picture of a dog for his birthday instead of the longed for flesh and blood dog. When Ben does acquire his live dog, there is still a sense of disappointment, for he finds, as his wise old granny said, that ' people get their heart's desire and then they have to begin to learn how to live with it '. Another gloomy birthday is described in *Seraphina*, by Mary K Harris. Poor, parentless Seraphina invents parents abroad for the edification of the other girls in the boarding house attached to her day school, and has to buy herself a parental birthday present to perpetuate the myth. Needless to say, her pretence cannot be maintained without discovery. In *Pappa Pellerin's daughter*, by Swedish Maria Gripe, the situation is reversed, as Loella has to buy a birthday present for her imaginary father. Sheena Porter vividly described the mother's birthday in *The bronze chrysanthemum*: the children's choice of gift, Jane's extra present, their plan to rise before their mother on her birthday and the celebratory family walk. An idyllic birthday was described by Noel Streatfeild in *The children on the top floor*, with full details of birthday presents and of a special outing. Another ideal birthday is marked by a grand party in *Charity at home*, by Barbara Willard. In American Virginia Sorensen's *Miracles on Maple Hill*, Marly gave Margie a friendship ring for her birthday, so Margie brings Marly one, and they swear to remain friends for ever.

In spite of various generalisations in critical writing about children's literature that parents, when present, play a more prominent role than before in family stories of the 1960's, this theory is only true with reservations. Parents may have been more active within the home in the 1960's, but examples of shared family outings are more conspicuous by their absence than by their presence. The sociologist might ask if this is a situation in real life reflected in children's books. It can reasonably be argued that children may not want to read of activities shared with parents, but may be more interested in reading about activities shared with their peers. If, however, family stories are intended to reflect aspects of real life, at least some of them must mention activities which involve both parents and children.

Few examples of family outings in the 1960's reveal the wealth of detail to be found in Eve Garnett's descriptions of the ' Bank holiday ' outing of more than thirty years ago in *The family from One End Street*: the saving up beforehand, the meticulous planning on an almost military scale for an outing to a seaside town only six miles from Otwell. Once the journey was safely accomplished, the day's pattern followed an intricate ritual: a walk along the promenade, a picnic on the beach, and then a leisurely parade along the pier. These activities were followed by paddling, watching Pierrots or a band, and ended with the burning problem of choosing a shanty for tea.

In *A dog so small*, A Philippa Pearce described various family outings: to see Oxford Street on Christmas Eve, to eat in a café, to visit the Tower of London. A family outing to the pantomime is described in *Charity at home*, by Barbara Willard. Both William Mayne's and Sheena Porter's families habitually go for walks.

Many outings in the 1960's did not include the entire family: three girls are invited to tea with an elderly lady in *The winter princess*, by Mary Treadgold, while a very awkward tea party is described by Geoffrey Trease in *The Maythorn story*. In the 1940's a novel approach to outings was taken by American Elizabeth Enright in *The Saturdays*: the Melendy children form a club, called ISAAC, which stands for Independent Saturday Afternoon Adventure Club. Each child has an independent outing of his or her own choice, before they unite for joint outings.

A search for relevant examples emphasises that to a large extent children and adults go their separate ways. In *Widdershins Crescent* by John Rowe Townsend, Sandra, Kevin, Harold and Jean are chased off on their own for a day's outing, and are quite satisfied with their picnic of meat pies, crisps and lemonade until they meet the two

Widdowson children, who come from a more prosperous home, and whose picnic offers a sharp contrast to that of the Thompson children. Kevin notices that ' it wasn't a bit like ours, in fact it was rather too fancy for my liking (not that I'd have refused it). They had a crusty foreign loaf, and butter in a little dish, and half a chicken, and some salad in a polythene bag, and hard-boiled eggs and biscuits and cheese and a bottle of milk '. In *Seraphina*, Mary K Harris brilliantly captured the awkwardness of Seraphina and Stephanie over Stephanie's visit to the aunt's house. In *The Thursday kidnapping*, by Antonia Forest, the two mothers spend a day shopping at the January sales, leaving the children to manage on their own. Margaret Storey reflected Pauline's blissful participation in peer activities with the Blacketts and their friends. William Mayne and Sheena Porter have been mentioned as writing about families sharing activities, but they have also been skilful in their presentation of incidents which include children without grown-ups: the restoration of the summer house in *The changeling*, or the children's camp in *Nordy Bank*.

Parents are sometimes more involved if the story centres round a holiday than if it takes place at home during term time, but it is dangerous always to make such an assertion. The 1930 type of holiday story was extended by Sheena Porter in *Nordy Bank*, but in *Cut off from crumpets* by Margaret J Baker, parents were very much in evidence. *Magnolia Buildings* by Elizabeth Stucley is unusual for its coverage of a family holiday in a holiday camp. William Mayne dealt with an unusual angle of town and country contrasts in *Summer visitors*—boys from a town school going to camp in the country. Noel Streatfeild chose a good approach for *The growing summer*, in which four children plunge to the depths of gloom, but also reach peaks of delight in the process of having to fend for themselves when they are sent to stay with Great-Aunt Dymphna for the summer. Vivid pictures of widely different Australian holidays, with parents very much in the background, are gained from *Patterson's Track*, or from *The green laurel*, both by Eleanor Spence, or from *Pastures of the blue crane*, by H F Brinsmead. The long dry summer in Jamaica is captured by Andrew Salkey in *Drought*, in which the anxieties of both the children and the adults are reflected. The acute boredom for a boy captive in New York during the summer is shared by the reader of *It's like this, cat* by Emily Cheney Neville. In *Wild goose summer* by P H Nortje, parents are very much involved in a story which contains one of the most barbaric incidents in current children's literature: the description of a baboon hunt.

The presentation of everyday life at home, or with the family outside the home, has so far been considered, but a large part of normal daily life is spent at school. This blend of home life and school life is far more frequently a natural feature of stories for children written in the 1960's, than in the pre-war period when the well known traditional school story, set in exclusive boarding school, catered for upper middle class children and satisfied less fortunate children's need for wish fulfilment. No more outstanding story of life in a girls' boarding school has been written since 1948 than Antonia Forest's *Autumn term*, which introduced the Marlow family, whose lives both at school and at home were successfully continued into the 1960's. William Mayne contributed to the boys' school story with *A swarm in May* in 1955 and its sequels, but it seems significant that no distinguished stories set entirely in boarding schools have appeared in the 1960's. The formula-type school story has gradually disappeared since the 1940's, to be replaced mainly with stories which reflect the more general reality for the majority, of a combination of home and day-school life.

Although in the 1960's few new stories were written entirely about life at school, in the same period, more brief, but telling details of school life of the period are interspersed with details of home life in books by William Mayne and Philip Turner, Mary K Harris and Margaret Storey.

This trend is also evident in books from abroad by Babbis Friis, Andrew Salkey, Eleanor Spence and other writers. The picture which fiction gives of school life must achieve a balance between impossible fantasy and the sheer hard work which may be involved in reality, and which is usually glossed over in fiction. There is too little handling of enthusiasms for particular subjects, in the manner achieved by writers like Mary K Harris or Barbara Willard, who have both written of teachers communicating a passion for their subjects to their pupils. Too much sport must make tedious reading for many children, and is perhaps a weakness in some of the works of both Antonia Forest and Philip Turner. In American family stories, references to baseball mean little to the British reader. In opposite circumstances, the same is true of cricket. In fiction, life at school appears to centre in a preponderance of books on extra-curricular rather than on curricular activities; drama, open days, sports and games, sales of work, clubs, appear to be more important than English, French or double maths.

It may reasonably be asked why there should not be emphasis on the lighter side of school life in fiction, but perhaps more than in any other area of everyday life, fiction tends to present a highly distorted reality. Teachers have occasionally been well presented— for example, by William Mayne in *Summer visitors*, by Andrew Salkey in *Drought*, by Ivan Southall in *Hills End*, and by Philip Turner in *Sea peril*. Readers are likely to remember Mr Holmes, the leader of the boys' camp in *Summer visitors*, Miss Carpenter's struggles to get qualified and her subsequent determination to teach in the Jamaican village of Nain, Miss Godwin's similarity to Miss Carpenter in her devotion to a small Australian town, and her passion for the dreary book she was writing about the mountains, Sandy's cordial relationship with David, Peter and Arthur in the pursuit of archeology. Mary K Harris created teachers with individual personalities: the ineffectual little teacher in *Jessica on her own*, the determined Miss Jason in *Seraphina* and the sympathetic Miss Maitland in *Penny's way*.

Authors frequently make no effort to conceal their contempt for some of the ridiculous rules and routines which are perpetrated for the sake of law, order and conformity. The trivia of the daily school routine have not been overlooked: journeys to school have been described by Maribel Edwin, Mary K Harris, Sheena Porter and Barbara Willard; the school dinner routine has been handled, sometimes opprobriously, by Honor Arundel, William Mayne and Noel Streatfeild, while even the ritual of school milk has been covered by Margaret Storey in *Pauline*. The true to life sparring between different schools was dealt with in the 1950's by Geoffrey Trease in his Bannermere series, and in the 1960's was skilfully manipulated by William Mayne in *Sand*.

In the stories of the 1960's, a remarkable proportion of school time appears to have been spent in visits to the headmaster or headmistress. They occur, for example, in books by Mary K Harris, William Mayne and John Rowe Townsend. In *Sand*, William Mayne gave a brilliant description of Ainsley's sensations as he waited with five friends for the headmaster's anger to erupt: 'Ainsley was last in, and he closed the door gently. He could not tell how much plus or minus there was in the Headmaster's voice. Ainsley thought that whatever it was, he was himself very much there and strangely awake'. He was intensely conscious of the most minute details of the Headmaster's room, from the blob of paint on the door handle to the shabby rug under the desk, but ' he knew that whatever he told himself about football matches was not true. His mind wanted to think of them, but something else, instinct perhaps, told him that there was trouble ahead '.

In the 1960's, the establishment of ' comprehensive ' schools became a controversial public issue, but the comprehensive school barely reached the children's stories of the period. A fleeting reference in Elfrida Vipont's *The pavilion* suggests that the idea of the comprehensive school will percolate into some of the stories of the 1970's. There may not have been library shelves of girls' or boys' school stories in the 1960's, as there were at least until the late 1940's, but stories of everyday life written in the 1950's and 1960's cumulatively give a more realistic picture of the day-school life experienced by the majority, than the fanciful tales of boarding schools so popular with earlier generations.

The best family stories reflect not only daily life at home and at school, but also a whole gamut of activities pursued by children: reading, acting, music and sports, going to the library, bird watching, ham radio, cars, ballet, riding, archeology or keeping pets. Reading about such activities in books is sometimes a vicarious means of fulfilment.

The books which are themselves mentioned in children's books provide fascinating sources of speculation, and it seems that they are frequently a reflection of authors' tastes and enthusiasms, rather than of objectivity, for the books which are mentioned do not correspond very closely to what is read in reality. Perhaps it is true to say that authors try to share their own enjoyable reading experiences with younger readers, forgetting that a new generation may not share their pleasure in older classics such as *The lamplighter,* by Maria Susanna Cummins or *Holiday House,* by Catherine Sinclair.

On the basis of the number of times he is quoted, a sociologist might conclude, quite wrongly, that British children read more Shakespeare than any other author. In the sample of books examined, the most regularly mentioned author after Shakespeare was Charles Dickens, followed by Jane Austen and the Brontës. Not only are the Brontës mentioned, but entire books set in the twentieth century revolve round some aspects of the Brontës' lives and works. Children's classics are regularly mentioned, but there are seldom references to current children's books: Arthur Ransome and Noel Streatfeild have been mentioned by later writers, but the most recent books mentioned are by C S Lewis, Mary Norton and Rosemary Sutcliff.

In view of both the increased concern over children's reading in the 1960's and the spread of information about children's books in the same period, it seems significant that any backwash of this has still to reach children's books. Perhaps by the end of the 1970's there will be references to William Mayne, A Philippa Pearce or K M Peyton, while new writers of the 1970's will probably be unmentioned. This potential means of firing a young reader's enthusiasm is either overlooked, or goes awry through an unwise choice of title. Sometimes a carefully planned choice of titles to be mentioned can be recognised: in *The gates of Bannerdale,* published in 1956, Geoffrey Trease referred to *Sinister Street* by Compton Mackenzie, and to *The scholar gipsy* by Matthew Arnold, both of which might be read with pleasure by a sixth-former looking forward to attending Oxford, although it is questionable whether sixth-formers would be reading the Bannermere series during either the 1950's or the 1960's. Antonia Forest's *Peter's room* is likely to encourage the young reader to find out more for himself about the lives and works of the Brontës.

The passion for writing which authors feel is reiterated again and again in their works, and is as much a spur to send the young reader scurrying for pen and paper, as the judicious mention of a book is likely to send him hastening to the library to borrow a copy. The writing urge has been reflected over the years in books from America and Canada, like *Little women* by Louisa M Alcott, or the Anne and Emily books by L M Montgomery; by the 1960's, authors as different as Ruth M Arthur, Elfrida Vipont and Eleanor Spence were creating characters whose determination to write must surely infect young readers.

Another deep interest which authors frequently attempt to share with young readers is a love of music. Kitty Barne successfully communicated the dedication necessary for a musical child in *She shall have music,* originally published in 1938, but wrote less skilfully of a musical family in *Musical honours,* first published in 1947. In the 1950's the most outstanding stories which reflected the strong influence of music were probably Elfrida Vipont's *The lark in the morn* and *The lark on the wing,* along with William Mayne's *A swarm in May* and *Chorister's cake.* In the 1960's Elfrida Vipont maintained the musical interest in *The pavilion.* Other writers of the 1960's who convey enthusiasm for music include Ruth M Arthur, Honor Arundel, Annabel Farjeon, Robina Beckles Willson, Americans Nat Hentoff and Virginia Sorensen, Australian H F Brinsmead and Italian Renée Reggiani. Composers are frequently mentioned: Bach, Beethoven, Brahms and Mozart, and more surprisingly perhaps, Janáček and Domenico Scarlatti. One device is difficulty in playing an instrument, and this situation has been handled by Annabel Farjeon and Priscilla M Warner. The achievement of one's own instrument has been described in *Beat of the city* by H F Brinsmead, in which Mary Laurel is trying to save up to buy a clarinet, and in *Miracles on Maple Hill,* by Virginia Sorensen, in which one of Joe's ambitions is to play in the school band. The choice of a career in jazz or in law is the gigantic problem facing Tom Curtis in *Jazz country,* by Nat Hentoff.

Pop music was skilfully handled by John Rowe Townsend in *The Hallersage sound,* although Aidan Chambers disputed the success of this in *The reluctant reader.* Pop was mentioned in *Magnolia Buildings,* by Elizabeth Stucley, before it had reached the significance which it gained in the later 1960's. Swedish Nan Inger actually mentioned the Beatles in *Katrin.* Dorothy Clewes and Robina Beckles Willson have both referred to concerts, and the latter is remarkable for her musical knowledge—in *Pineapple Palace* she describes conducting, performing, composing, musical lectures, unusual musical instruments, examining in music, musical festivals, and works by various composers. In some family stories, an attribute of the mother may be the ability to play a musical instrument: the formidable mother in *Midway* by Anne Barrett plays the piano; the mother in *Castaway Christmas* by Margaret J Baker is a concert pianist; while the mother in Elfrida Vipont's *The spring of the year*, published in 1957, and in its 1960 sequel, *Flowering spring*, is both a flautist and a violinist. An unusual slant to the musical angle was given by Renée Reggiani in *The adventures of five children and a dog*: Turi wins a bandmaster scholarship to Milan, and the children he has trained to form his little band, are so devoted that they follow him to Milan. It is debatable, however, whether musical children always want to read about music, rather than actively participate in musical activities.

This is equally true of acting, which was enthusiastically described by Noel Streatfeild in the 1930's, by Pamela Brown in the 1940's, by Geoffrey Trease in the 1950's and by Elfrida Vipont in the 1960's.

Before the 1960's, there were few references to public libraries in children's books. It is interesting to consider whether the increasing mention of them during the 1960's reflected increased library consciousness on the part of authors or on the part of children. It is noticeable that the public library was often mentioned in American children's books from the 1930's, and in a more favourable guise than is usually shown in British children's books, from which a depressing picture emerges—even at the end of the 1960's—of chocolate brown paint, rigidly enforced silence, poor relationships between librarians and readers, and of the library as a refuge for poor old men with nowhere else to go. Librarians must feel anything but flattered at the image which emerges from books by A Philippa Pearce, Mary K Harris or Eleanor Spence. In *A dog so small* by Philippa Pearce, the library assistant is very unenthusiastic about allowing Ben to look at books about dogs in the adult library; in Australia, Eleanor Spence wrote, in *The year of the currawong*, that 'Alex liked the library. It was an old one-storeyed building, part sandstone and part brick, set in a square of lawn edged with yellow-spiked flax-bushes and formal aloes. Inside it was quiet and tranquil and filled with the mixed smells of books and floor wax and glue. " The children's library is through the other door," said the girl at the main desk. "I know," said Alex politely. "But I'm looking for some books or papers about the history of mining . . .".' In the end the librarian's enthusiasm equals Alex's and she is a real help to him.

One of the most recurring interests in stories of everyday life lies in pets, from ordinary cats and dogs to more exotic horses, or even falcons. The interest in pets and animals occurs in books from all parts of the world, and is remarkable for the strong emotions it can arouse. Any theory that an interest in pets is a peculiarly British characteristic is disproved by the number of stories from other countries which reflect a strong interest in some species of animal: *It's like this, cat,* by American Emily Cheney Neville; *Za the truffle boy,* by Angela Latini; *The Bates family,* by Australian Reginald Ottley, and *The Cloud with the silver lining,* by Jamaican C Everard Palmer. A pet's integral part in the family is a basic feature of books by Margaret J Baker, Sheena Porter or Jenifer Wayne. In their handling of pets, most authors show a commendably realistic approach, and do not simplify the difficulties which pets can cause. Chapter four attempts to explain how pets are frequently used for a type of wish fulfilment theme, rather than as a reflection of reality, in books like *A dog so small* by A Philippa Pearce and *Fly-by-night* by K M Peyton, which both bring out the enormous gulf between the dream and the reality.

The inevitable conclusion to be reached from the details of everyday life given in family stories of the 1960's is not that the family activities were peculiar to the 1960's, but that they were generally the opposite: getting up, having breakfast, helping at home, going to school, returning home after school, doing homework, having family meals, seeing friends or pursuing some interest or hobby before going to bed. This widespread routine appears to be broken mainly by weekends, or by special occasions, visits, outings or holidays.

In *The school librarian,* December 1962, J K G Taylor compared family stories of the 1930's and 1950's in his article on 'The social background of children's fiction', and expressed concern over the paucity of references to current affairs, particularly in the 1930's. It is doubtful whether the family stories of the 1960's give more references to topical matters than their counterparts of the 1950's, but it must of course be remembered that the main disadvantage of contemporary allusions is that they can date a book very rapidly. Authors are perhaps wiser to concentrate on timeless issues if they wish their books to last. During the 1960's, young readers of family stories originally published in the 1930's and 1940's must have found it hard to understand the references to bakelite, silk stockings, ration books or sweet coupons, *new* twelve sided threepenny bits, *Rainbow* or *Chicks own* comics, American dance music, or even Hitler. Ten years hence it is questionable whether young readers will appreciate the references in family stories of the 1960's to the Beatles, Tommy Steele, Elvis Presley, Richard Dimbleby, *Coronation Street,* and heroin smuggling.

During the 1960's, television appears to have been one of the most general influences, both in fiction and in reality, judging from its regular mention in family stories of the period: programmes, personalities, techniques and television sets are all treated with a surprising degree of earnestness. Apart from the British Broadcasting Corporation, the Royal Society for the Prevention of Cruelty to Animals, the Automobile Association, the Royal Air Force, and the United Nations Organisation have all been mentioned in various family stories of the 1960's. The National Health Service was occasionally mentioned, and this may have been a reflection of the part it has come to play in reality. In *The toppling Towers,* Barbara Willard boldly mentioned several vital issues of the late 1960's: industrial relations, a take-over bid, racial integration, and even Vietnam. The majority of authors tend to present a more blurred contemporary scene, and in the 1960's, current affairs were generally as tenuously handled as in the 1930's.

Other patterns emerge in the coverage of everyday life in family stories of the 1960's: the still cursory treatment of parents; the sharing of interests and enthusiasms; the wider picture of family life throughout the world; the scarcity of material about average British life; the acute danger of preoccupation with working class life at a very low level; and the signs of an overwhelming sense of sociological purpose. Parents, if alive, may have been more involved in family life within the home, but only occasionally participate in joint family activities such as outings and visits, which makes the reader wonder whether family stories of the 1960's were reflecting reality in this respect, or whether they were clinging to the tradition of parents who are in evidence as little as possible.

Whether in general the family stories of the 1960's accurately reflect life of the period is a thorny question. Some writers, like Gillian Avery, Hester Burton, John Rowe Townsend, Jill Paton Walsh and Americans Frances Litt Brown and Robert Burch, have, of course, sometimes chosen an earlier decade for the setting of their family stories, and it also seems reasonable to say that most writers reflect at least slightly earlier periods than their dates of publication. This study is concerned with books published in Britain in the 1960's, which may not always give a strict interpretation of life in the 1960's. It will be interesting to see whether in the 1970's any counterbalancing trend develops to limit the amount of material about dreary, often hopeless working class backgrounds, and to provide more non-denominational material and less didacticism.

PROBLEMS

The family story must be about life within or beyond the bounds of reality, within or beyond a young reader's experience. If it is to reflect real life at all, the family story must include problems. The story may revolve around family events, or around a family's burning interest in some topic, but in most family stories at least one problem is inevitable if not also pertinent to the pattern of the story.

Besides the passive reflection of reality, problems are also used to satisfy a child's needs for wish fulfilment and for challenge. The presentation of problems can be of practical help to the child confronted with what Joan Cass described in *Literature and the young child* (Longmans, 1967), as 'the intensely hostile impulses that children often experience towards each other, even in the best brought up families'. Often, only forthright handling in family stories of such problems as jealousy, rivalry, ambivalent feelings towards parents and siblings can make a child realise that his apparently shameful feelings are not unique. Joan Cass also suggested that stories of a reasonably normal family life, which must therefore inevitably include occasional problems, have a contribution to make

58

to children deprived of normal home life. It might also be said that in current family stories, an author's urge to instruct young readers can be satisfied if he attempts to handle either one main problem or a number of lesser problems. It is true that a variety of different problems gives a more accurate reflection of real life, but the opportunity to handle one problem in depth can be more useful than cursory treatment of several.

In her introduction to *The best children's books of 1966*, Naomi Lewis expressed the view that 'identification is far more effective than crude admonishment in waking imagination', but the tempting desire to moralise is almost too obvious in a book like *Beat of the city*, by Australian H F Brinsmead. In the successful handling of problems, authors have to avoid not only an over-didactic tone, but also any likelihood of contributing to the deterioration of a difficult situation in real life. *The owl in the barn* by Charlotte Hough, for example, presents an unsatisfactory adoption situation and then offers a solution to it which is unlikely to occur in real life, as the unhappy adopted child Grizelda discovers her real father. Again, *Ginger and number 10* by Prudence Andrew covers delicate ground on the racial question, and seems hardly likely to improve a tricky situation in real life.

Problems in children's family stories cover a wide ground, and a list of them tackled by writers during the 1960's would include at least the following topics: difficulties involving the entire family or individual members over sickness, finances, a change of environment; more dramatic family difficulties caused by flood, hurricane or other disaster, or by the threat of change by government planners; problems resulting from mother at work, from the remarriage of widowed parents, from the divorce or separation of parents or from the death of parents; strife between members of the family over attitudes, habits or feelings, over the choice of career or friends, over pets; problems of other countries; current issues on such topics as teenagers, racial integration, disabled children, old people, illegitimacy, education. The range is considerable. Areas which all parents realise may create problems include starting school, going to hospital, accepting a new baby, or a new parent; but the adult also has to remember that a problem which seems insignificant to him may have disproportionate significance for a child: the accomplishment of an unfamiliar task, the undertaking of a solitary journey, the confession of a minor misdeed. More alarming still are the childish problems of which the unsuspecting adult is totally unaware.

Ideally, a story of this kind should show how a child or a family deal with a crisis, and the crisis should be worth the pursuit. Ruth M Arthur, Honor Arundel, John Rowe Townsend and Barbara Willard are some of the authors who deal with problems which arise as a result of new environment. Richard Parker, K M Peyton and Sheena Porter support families rallied together against the government planners of the sixties, a theme also used by Barbara Willard in the late 1950's. The popular problem of flooding, a disagreeable experience in reality, occurred as early as 1937 in *Jam tomorrow,* by Monica Redlich, but was more adroitly handled in the 1960's by Hester Burton in *The great gale,* and by Margaret J Baker in *Castaway Christmas.* Hazards from severe falls of snow cause problems in *Cut off from crumpets,* also by Margaret J Baker, in *The snowbound bus* by Maribel Edwin, and in *Ladder to the sky* by American Ruth Forbes Chandler. Problems which the elements cause in other countries include Australian bush fires, covered by Ivan Southall in *Ash Road,* and hurricane and drought, both treated by Andrew Salkey in books with those titles. In many cases the critic might question the moral value of the crisis handled, but the pursuit is amply justified in books of the quality of *The plan for Birdsmarsh* by K M Peyton, *Berries Goodman* by American Emily Cheney Neville, *The green laurel* by Australian Eleanor Spence, or *Hurricane* by Andrew Salkey.

The treatment of a problem should increase a child's understanding and put the problem in perspective for him, according to Geoffrey Trease, who successfully put his theories into practice with the Bannermere series in the late 1940's and 1950's, and with the Maythorn books in the 1960's. In *Intent upon reading,* Margery Fisher's view was that family stories should show 'testing in ordinary situations', a tenet followed by writers of the calibre of John Rowe Townsend and Barbara Willard; but in the 1960's, writers including Margaret J Baker, Anne Barrett, K M Peyton, Sheena Porter, Australians H F Brinsmead and Ivan Southall were all more adept at portraying testing in *extraordinary* situations.

Problems which satisfy a child's need for wish fulfilment with the well-used themes of running away, being lost, being involved in a search, or possessing one's own hideaway or 'den' are less vital, although often enjoyable. Authors who take this line may not concentrate on more basic personal problems, but often succeed in giving convincing details of family life in spite of sometimes far-fetched plots. Authors may have idealistic theories about the presentation of problems in children's fiction as a means of helping children to solve similar problems in real life, but in *Margin for surprise*, Ruth Hill Viguers stated categorically that a child 'does not have to have books angled at his specific problems or needs', which may strike some adults as an extreme point of view. This opinion is difficult to accept entirely, especially for parents with children today, who tend to be more aware of the difficulties which children encounter, some perennial and some peculiar to each decade. These problems deserved at least some coverage in the books of the 1960's, but, regrettably, in many cases did not receive it.

Although writers in the 1960's showed in general more knowledge of current problems than their predecessors, many areas were neglected or ignored. Writers in the 1930's clearly showed a singular unawareness of the problems of their period. J K G Taylor has said that in children's books of the 1930's 'parents portrayed at home are feeling the economic pinch, but bravely applying themselves to the task of maintaining their faithful retainers and meeting the school fees'! In *Strangers at the Farm School*, published in 1940, Josephine Elder dealt, by contrast, with the problems of Jewish children exiled from Germany in the 1930's, and in doing so, handled an unusual theme at a time when school stories were almost exclusively devoted to rivalries, feuds, mysteries or 'midnight feasts'. The formula type of school story was almost exhausted by the 1950's, and convincingly realistic problems were considered in some of the stories of Mary K Harris, E W Hildick, William Mayne or Margaret Storey, in which home and school life of the 1950's and 1960's were simultaneously part of one pattern.

Eve Garnett dealt with working class dilemmas of the 1930's, from shoes frequently in need of repair to a lost grammar school hat; but in the 1960's, a number of writers, particularly John Rowe

Townsend and Elizabeth Stucley, covered current working class difficulties relating to jobs, houses, weekly bills, hire purchase payments, clothes, gangs and delinquency.

Nowadays, fortunately, there is no sense of inferiority attached to day school, to having a mother at work, or to juvenile employment after school hours. In the 1930's, less realistic treatments related to holidays were the pivots of books by Arthur Ransome, M E Atkinson, Kathleen Hull and Pamela Whitlock and Aubrey de Selincourt. The well-worn holiday theme was used by Noel Streatfeild in the 1960's: *The growing summer* offers a down-to-earth account of the practical difficulties for four children unused to fending for themselves, caused by hiding a mysterious boy in their great-aunt's house.

The scarcity in the 1930's of material related to the real life of a large majority of children may partially account for the reputation enjoyed by *The family from One End Street* by Eve Garnett, and may also be the cause of the preponderance of stories about contemporary life awarded the Library Association's Carnegie medal between 1936 and 1941. Writers of this type of book included Arthur Ransome, Eve Garnett, Noel Streatfeild, Kitty Barne and Mary Treadgold, but with the exception of Eve Garnett, these writers all dealt with a way of life unfamiliar to a large proportion of children, both in the 1930's and today.

The second world war provided less material for writers of children's books than might have been expected, the most important examples from the period being *Visitors from London* and *We'll meet in England,* both by Kitty Barne, *The children of Primrose Lane* by Noel Streatfeild, and *We couldn't leave Dinah* by Mary Treadgold. In the 1960's two writers found the war a rich source of inspiration: Hester Burton and Jill Paton Walsh, whose books *In spite of all terror* and *The Dolphin crossing,* both more vivid than the books written earlier, are now historical novels rather than family stories of the 1960's, since both deal with problems resulting from the war. J K G Taylor considered that by the 1950's a new formula had developed, with an historical theme used against a contemporary background. The problems involved in such situations were successfully shown in the 1960's by writers of the quality of Alan Garner, William Mayne, Sheena Porter or Eleanor Spence.

It is appropriate to consider to what extent problems handled in current children's books are relevant to the 1960's. Some problems are ageless: the death of parents, adjusting to the remarriage of a remaining parent, strife with either parents or siblings; but if an armful of books indicates a trend, the 1960's showed a developing consciousness of current problems: the increase in the number of mothers at work, in the number of illegitimate children, in the number of children with physical or mental defects, the racial issue, the higher divorce rate. Yet important areas were neglected or ignored: there was a conspicuous lack of adequate coverage of the problems of teenagers; there was little attempt to handle seriously attitudes to religion or to social situations of the 1960's. Although it has been argued that authors must avoid an obviously didactic or moralistic approach, the harsher problems can be successfully handled, and have to be faced in literature as in reality. No account of the family story of the 1960's would be complete without a glance at some of the ways in which authors were presenting these issues.

In real life debate is rife whether mothers should work outside the home. Some of those in favour point out that it is more desirable to have a contented mother working outside the home than a frustrated housebound mother; that the wider interests of mothers at work are beneficial to the children; that the larger income is desirable, even if not always essential, and that children in these circumstances are more appreciative of the mother. Those who argue against mothers at work emphasise the uncertainties and incontinuity of domestic arrangements; the weariness of the mother on return home after a day's work; the absorption of the increased income in personal expenses for the mother, in more expensive housekeeping and in domestic help, if available. Insecurity of the children of mothers at work is often mentioned also, although various surveys insist that there is no proof of this. But unarguably essential if a mother is out at work, is some adequate alternative form of domestic arrangement. As some stories show, in reality there is often *no* outside help, children have to do the chores (not necessarily a bad thing), and children are all too likely to feel at a loose end in the absence of mother. These contingencies all arose in *The latchkey children,* by Eric Allen, in which three of the mothers are engaged in a launderette, an agency for servants and an office respectively. In a story like *The hunt for Harry*, Rosemary Weir solved the problems of the family of a glamorous actress by the appearance of an aunt who was willing to take over the domestic front: a solution more likely in fiction than in reality. In *Midway* by Anne Barrett, an ex-ballet dancer is in charge of the domestic arrangements, while the exotic mother is likened to the ' little red line that ran perpetually round the electricity meter '. This overpowering mother is a pianist, paints, exhibits, gives lessons at home, sews dresses and cooks unusual dishes. It was also pointed out that she was an embarrassment at school functions! No wonder that Mark, the middle one of a talented family feels very inferior to both parents and siblings.

Having given examples of domestic arrangements with mother at work, it is only fair to mention that life is not necessarily idyllic with mother at home. In *Clemence and Ginger* by Jenifer Wayne, the mother writes to earn extra money, but the housekeeping is chaotic; the harassed mother in *Penny's way* by Mary K Harris struggles to cope with her three daughters. *Clemence and Ginger* and *The latchkey children* emphasised the material advantages of having the mother at work, but the so-called intangible ' benefits ' are harder to find. Other stories such as *The winter princess* by Mary Treadgold reflected the delight of a child when her working mother was at home to produce hot ginger bread with ice cream, or to whisk up a ' flamingo-pink jelly '.

American stories reflect the trend of mothers at work outside the home, while Australian stories give pictures both of mothers at work outside the home and heavily overworked at home. In *Katrin*, Swedish Nan Inger pinpointed some of the apparently insoluble difficulties, particularly that of finding a suitable substitute for the mother. Another Swede, Maria Gripe, gave an extreme picture of an irresponsible mother at work in *Pappa Pellerin's daughter*. In this book, the mother, a ship's cook, goes to America for a year to earn a lot of money, which causes her daughter Loella considerable unhappiness. From whichever country it comes, the children's fiction, like reality, shows that a satisfactory home life with mother out at work is hard to achieve.

The divorce or separation of parents was only rarely considered by writers for children in the 1960's. This could be partly attributed to the painfulness of the situation, but in an age of rising divorce rates, there is surely some need for stories which honestly attempt to deal with some of the issues. *Cut off from crumpets* by Margaret J Baker is one of the few books which brings out credibly the suffering of two children over their parents' separation. Letty, the daughter involved, thought that ' the adult world in which her parents had quarrelled and parted had towered over them both. Icy cliffs had closed them in. Nothing she and Owen said or did could make any changes in that grown up world. Most of the things which had gone wrong they could not understand. The problems belonged to their parents. She and Owen had not power to solve them, however much they longed to do so. The only sensible thing to do was to leave their parents alone '.

In 1959 Antonia Forest wrote briefly in *End of term* of the problems of Esther, whose mother had been divorced and remarries. In *Dragon summer*, Ruth M Arthur succeeded in reflecting the miseries of both mother and daughter after the parents have been divorced. Another approach was taken by Ivan Southall in *Finn's Folly*: Alison is left in the care of her father at the age of four, when the mother leaves them. By contrast, an almost humorous attitude to divorce was taken in *The Seventeenth Street gang*, by Emily Cheney Neville. Toby Meyer's parents are divorced, a situation which Toby finds acceptable for most of the time, as it means double outings, but she does not appreciate the interminable rows by telephone.

Another current issue slowly finding discussion in children's books is the racial question. In both *How many miles to Babylon?* by Paula Fox and *Jennifer, Hecate, Macbeth and me* by Mrs E L Konigsburg, the reader only finds out accidentally that James and Jennifer are coloured children. In *The Seventeenth Street gang* by Emily Cheney Neville, an equally casual reference revealed that Junior is Puerto Rican. An American story which made no attempt to gloss over the difficulties was *Ladder to the sky* by Ruth Forbes Chandler, which shows a whole range of problems, faced by Chip Wood and his family because of their colour. The story was weakened by the contrivance of a artificially villainous white family.

In this country a mere handful of books mention the issue. In this context *Ginger and number 10* by Prudence Andrew has already been questioned, for it states clearly the disagreeable prejudices of an older generation, which there seems no real need for the younger reader to meet. This author also gave an uncomfortably convincing picture of the squalor, and also the verve, of the lives of the nine West Indians who came to live in Ginger's street. Although the problem of integration was provisionally solved by the end of the book, the reader cannot help wondering whether the same situation would have worked out as satisfactorily in real life. Richard Parker gave a touching picture of a little Indian girl, Rain, in *The boy who wasn't lonely*. Rosemary Weir tackled some of the difficulties in *The hunt for Harry*, but Ruth M Arthur barely scratched the surface of the problem in *Portrait of Margarita*. Eric Allen matter-of-factly introduced a West Indian boy in *The latchkey children*. In *The rolling season* by William Mayne, a West Indian bus conductor, Profound d Pew, has been in England for six years, and although he considers himself a city dweller, is adjusting, with his English wife, to life in the Wiltshire village of Bourne Bridge. Josephine Kamm boldly dealt with the problems of a teenage girl's relationship with a boy from British Guiana in *Out of step*. Stories from India or Jamaica may, quite rightly, not even mention the colour question, but the South African story, *Wild Goose summer* by P H Nortje, gave a somewhat condescending description to multi-racial eyes of a non-European boy, Jakob: 'Long ago I had learnt that it could be dangerous to rely on Jakob's brain—in a moment of emergency he could never think up a feasible plan. He made up for this more than twice over, however, by offering me without reservation everything he had. His eternal good nature, his endless patience, and his blind faith made him a wonderful accomplice'.

Adoption is a topic which appears to have occurred more frequently in the last few years. This could reflect a general increase in the illegitimacy rate, but a more plausible opinion may be that of a writer in the *Times literary supplement*, November 26 1964, who wrote that 'the appeal of foundling status is strong for the over-secure'. The problems arising from adoption were handled in different ways by Josephine Kamm in *No strangers here;* by Ruth M Arthur in *Requiem for a princess* and by Tasmanian Nan Chauncy in *Lizzie Lights*. Each of these books revealed the violent reactions of three girls who only discovered in their teens that they had been adopted. A calmer account of adoption was given in *Beat of the city* by H F Brinsmead, whose sensible character Jason Brown, a lorry driver and an over-gentle ' bouncer ', went to the Laurel family on the death of his drunken father, and was later adopted by them. *Portrait of Margarita* by Ruth M Arthur and *Pineapple Palace* by Robina Beckles Willson both mentioned adoption offhandedly, showing a diametrically opposed reaction to that of the girls in *No strangers here, Requiem for a princess,* and *Lizzie Lights.* The fostering angle was considered by Richard Parker in *Second-hand family,* which showed how Giles adjusts to life with a less than ideal foster family. An unusual view of fostering was given in *Fly-by-night,* by K M Peyton.

The problems of the handicapped or sick child are rarely tackled, in spite of the number of children with disabilities. E W Hildick has already been mentioned as describing friendship kept up in circumstances of ill health. He used this theme both in *The questers* and in *The boy at the window.* In *Portrait of Margarita,* Ruth M Arthur dwelt briefly, but sensitively on the grave problems of an autistic child and her family. Dorothy Clewes was concerned over the problems of a teenage boy blinded in an accident in her book *Guide dog.* Veronica Robinson undertook considerable research on the deaf for her novel *David in silence,* which is likely to make normal children more aware of the difficulties facing deaf children. In *Colonel Sheperton's clock,* David is lame, and Philip Turner wrote that ' when you are still small, you are unsteady on your legs anyway, and you cannot do much. But as you get older, more and more activities become possible. But not for David. He felt like a wild goose tethered by the leg, unable to answer the call of his kind, and his father did not notice '.

Kersti, by Norwegian Babbis Friis, is written for older girls, and deals with the problems of a five year old girl who has been badly scarred in an accident. Adults were totally unaware of some of the poor child's suffering at the hands of heartless children. In *Finn's Folly,* Ivan Southall painted a sombre picture of a family whose life had to be geared to the needs of the youngest child, David, a mongol. But a more cheerful picture was given by another Australian, Patricia Wrightson, in *' I own the racecourse!',* which centred around a backward boy Andy, accepted and cared for by his contemporaries. In *Rossie*, set in America in the 1930's, Dutch A Rutgers van der Loeff gave a frank picture of the suffering caused by burns. Books covering the problems mentioned were exceptions in the 1960's, and authors have still to recognise that this kind of story has a valuable contribution to make to children's development, by making normal children aware of problems far more complex than their own. They not only increase awareness of the situations of others, but arouse sympathy, tolerance, and where relevant, a desire to help.

Less obvious disabilities, still crippling to those afflicted, deserve attention from children's writers. In *Ginger and number 10*, Prudence Andrew demonstrated Odya's inability to read properly, and reported how he read a passage from *The highwayman* by Henry Newbolt omitting all the words he did not know. The reader, irritated by this incident, is later mollified when Odya has reading sessions in the shed which Andy's father allows the boys to use. Reading difficulties were also handled by Alice Lunt in *Eileen of Redstone Farm*, and by American Robert Burch in *Skinny*. *Za the truffle boy*, by Italian Angela Latini, tells of Za's grandmother learning to read, and of her sense of achievement when she eventually succeeds. As fifteen percent of school children in the UK are thought to leave school unable to read adequately, this is a problem that merits some attention, if only to inspire the more literate to help.

In an age when older people enjoy a longer expectation of life than ever before, children's understanding and sympathy for an older generation can be increased through the example of books. The problems of older people are briefly mentioned in *Jessica on her own* by Mary K Harris, while in the 1950's Diana Pullein-Thompson wrote *The boy and the donkey*, which gave a realistic picture of the problems of Old Jock, a rag and bone man, who is helped over a difficult period by ten year old Duggie. In *Ollie*, by Jenifer Wayne, the children suddenly realise that their elderly friend, Miss Diamond, must be in financial difficulties, and they try to help her, with a success unlikely to be paralleled in reality. In *It's like this, cat*, Emily Cheney Neville drew a most understanding picture of an old lady, Kate, and her numerous cats. She provides comfort for Dave when relations are uncomfortably strained at home. Another down-to-earth approach was made by Ivan Southall in *Ash Road,* in which he described Grandpa Tanner, whose wife has been dead for many years: 'there was not much left for Grandpa, really, except the routine of getting up and going to bed, and remembering'. In *The cloud with the silver lining* by Jamaican author C Everard Palmer, the grandsons realised the need for their grandfather to find a purpose in life after his leg has been amputated, and successfully set about rehabilitating him. On returning to the scene of his boyhood, another grandfather gains a new lease of life in *Pastures of the blue crane* by Australian H F Brinsmead.

The particular problems of teenagers were rarely handled with any depth in the 1960's. In *Written for children,* John Rowe Townsend gave a useful summary of problems of teenagers which need coverage: 'there are matters such as starting work (or staying at school), striking out new relationships with parents and with the adult world, coming to terms with the opposite sex, and above all discovering what kind of person you really are, that are of utmost interest to adolescents but that are not often dealt with in adult fiction, or at least not dealt with in ways that seem helpful'. The Americans have for years shown more awareness of the teenage dilemma with writers like Mary Stolz boldly attempting to search the difficulties of growing up and the sudden unleashing of unexpected emotions.

Even in America, however, there is little cause for complacency about the present material dealing with teenage problems. James Steel Smith wrote in *A critical approach to children's literature* that 'domestic fiction for adolescents is and always has been in a sad state. This is one of the few areas of non adult literature that has failed to produce much literature of value beyond the immediate satisfaction of the needs of its age group'. In British writing there tends to be an enormous gulf between fiction and reality. *Pineapple Palace* by Robina Beckles Willson shows no indication of her teenagers of opposite sexes feeling any sexually-based awareness of each other. But *Islands of strangers* by George Beardmore touches very delicately on two teenagers slowly developing feelings for each other, and *The two sisters* by Honor Arundel is unusual in that it approaches the problems of a teenage marriage, though the problems are not examined in any depth.

The scapegoat by Sheena Porter reflected trends of the 1960's in its lesser details of the elder sister Ruth's friendship with the boy Clive. *Hell's Edge,* and its sequel *The Hallersage sound* by John Rowe Townsend, attempted, within limits, to give convincing details of teenage relationships. In *Emma's island,* the sequel to *The high house* by Honor Arundel, the author was unusually forthright for a writer for teenagers, in her descriptions of Emma's experiences of the opposite sex. It is hardly an excess of romantic writing to have Emma describe a kiss as ' uncomfortable (because I had been taken unawares) and my nose was squashed up against his cheek so that it was almost impossible to breathe '.

American attitudes to teenage problems are often more realistic. In *It's like this, cat,* Emily Cheney Neville showed the petrifying shyness of Dave when faced with teenage girls, a feeling shared by the two boys in *Wild goose summer* by South African P H Nortje. In *The Seventeenth Street gang,* Emily Cheney Neville depicted the over-anxious mother trying to hasten the formation of a boy/girl relationship. *Beyond the jungle,* a moving autobiographical novel by Sita Rathnamal, dealt acutely with the uncontrollable feelings of an Indian girl.

Thus far, different types of problem have been briefly considered. It is also relevant to examine how different authors attempted to present problems, whether they offered solutions, and whether they achieved any success. Some books may revolve around a single major problem, although minor problems may also occur. This could be said of *The latchkey children* by Eric Allen, in which the main problem is that facing children left on their own while mothers are at work. The same is true of *Cut off from crumpets* by Margaret J Baker, which deals with the severe winter of 1963, and of *Three and one to carry* by Barbara Willard, in which the central problem is the assimilation of an unwanted boy into the family, and of *The scapegoat* by Sheena Porter, in which the basic problem is the non-acceptance by Carys of her stepmother.

Concentration on one main problem tends to be more successful than mere superficial handling of a series of problems. Authors like Ruth M Arthur and Mary K Harris offered books which bristled with problems: in *Portrait of Margarita*, Ruth M Arthur included problems relating to the death of parents, falling in love with an older man, an autistic child, adoption, colour, jealousy—all themes worthy of fuller treatment. Similarly, in *Seraphina*, Mary K Harris presented the death of a grandmother, missing parents, an incompatible aunt, deceit, lack of money, personal misunderstandings, while in *Jessica on her own*, the differences of three sisters, the adjustment of an orphan cousin, an unacceptable friendship (from the parents' point of view) between Jessica and a dustman's daughter, privations of old people, the implications of the Freedom-from-Hunger movement, an unemployed uncle, a teacher ineffectually trying to control her class, were some of the numerous situations raised, though not developed in detail.

In American books, some of the problems may be peculiarly American, but many are universal. Emily Cheney Neville concentrated on anti-semitism in *Berries Goodman*, but included a wider variety of issues in *It's like this, cat* and in *The Seventeenth Street gang*. The central problem in *Miracles on Maple Hill* by Virginia Sorensen was the readjustment of the father to ordinary life after the second world war, while Joseph Krumgold covered a variety of problems in *Onion John*, but was particularly concerned over the repercussions in a small town when the citizens try to alter the way of life of an eccentric inhabitant. Problems encountered in other environments and societies were well handled by H F Brinsmead, Joan Phipson, Ivan Southall, Eleanor Spence, Andrew Salkey, C Everard Palmer and P H Nortje. It is particularly interesting for a child reader to see in books from other countries the universality of many of the human problems with which he himself is familiar.

Finally, there is another category of problem which greatly appeals to young readers: that of wish fulfilment, of which at least five thematic variations are frequently used, sometimes in conjunction with more realistic problems, and sometimes independently. The main variations are the run away child, or, from another angle, the lost child; possession of an animal or of a place (room, hut, house); a search for something or someone. In 1948 Geoffrey Trease commented in his book *Tales out of school* on the high incidence of fictional running away, but it was still high in the 1960's and occurred in a large number of stories, including *The scapegoat* by Sheena Porter, *Pauline* by Margaret Storey, and *Duck on a pond* by Barbara Willard. Running away was as common in Australian material of the 1960's as in British, being somewhat overworked by Eleanor Spence in *Patterson's Track*, in which there were three cases of running away in one story. Margery Fisher stated her belief that children's innate desire for independence ' accounts for the popularity of stories about running away—about children on their own '. She went on to say that the value of the running away themes is that there is ' safety in the end, no matter what hazards they describe first '.

The lost child situation occurred in *The bus girls* by Mary K Harris, in *The Thursday kidnapping* by Antonia Forest, and in *Deerfold* by Sheena Porter. In books dealing with running away or being lost, authors usually emphasised the anguish of parents and adults over the missing child. The Americans also enjoy these themes, a supreme example being *From the mixed-up files of Mrs Basil E Frankweiler* by Mrs E L Konigsburg, in which a brother and sister successfully organise an expedition to the Metropolitan Museum in New York and live there undetected for several days. Before the 1960's, in *The Saturdays* by Elizabeth Enright, comfortable Cuffy, who is the substitute for mother, says ' I suppose I can't keep you from getting a little lost once in a while. It'd be against nature '.

The idea of a place of one's own, however small, appears to have a perennial appeal for the child. In the opening chapter of *The Saturdays*, a satisfyingly detailed description is given of the Melendy children's ' office ' at the top of the house: a room full of junk in which there are no unnecessary grown up restrictions. In another American story, *Ladder to the sky* by Ruth Forbes Chandler, Chip has his own den in a room over the barn. The idea of such a refuge must have had a painful appeal to the regimented child of the 1960's living in smaller, modern houses and required to keep his possessions tidy and to restrict his activities in his family's one public through-room.

More ambitious ' places ' were offered by some writers: a deserted house, Cendlings, is the children's haunt in *Tansy of Tring Street* by Mabel Esther Allan; a disused cottage is restored by the children in *The Paradise summer* by Priscilla M Warner; an old summer house is taken over by the children in *The changeling* by William Mayne; a shed is the refuge in *The linhay on Hunter's Hill* by Lois Lamplugh; both a deserted house and an empty 'funhouse' provide shelters for the boys in *How many miles to Babylon?* by American Paula Fox. In the 1950's, Tessie had her own caravan in *Tessie growing up* by Priscilla M Warner, a theme also used in the 1930's, by M E Atkinson in *August adventure,* and by Howard Spring in *Sampson's Circus.* Possession of one's own place usually involves problems of some kind, often of maintaining secrecy or of putting the place in order.

The desire for an animal of one's own was another well-used theme in the 1960's, which offered a diversity of problems. Dogs were the sources of trouble in *A dog so small* by A Philippa Pearce, *Nordy Bank* by Sheena Porter, and *The linhay on Hunter's Hill* by Lois Lamplugh; cats created the difficulties in *No one must know* by Barbara Sleigh, birds in *Duck on a pond* by Barbara Willard, horses in *Fly-by-night* by K M Peyton, and in *The Lord Mayor's show* by Vian Smith.

The search theme and its problems have been effectively handled by authors who include Alan Garner, William Mayne, Sheena Porter, H F Brinsmead and Eleanor Spence. In the 1960's, a trend from the 1950's towards search with an archeological or historical foundation was continued, and in several instances this interest is likely to make books with a contemporary setting more enduring than books concerned solely with current issues. Similarly, some fantasies in a 1960's setting may survive rather because of the fantasy than because of the setting.

Authors may have succeeded in presenting a greater variety of problems than their counterparts of thirty years ago, but it appeared to be easier to offer the problems than to provide realistic solutions. Problems were frequently more conveniently solved in fiction than in reality. It would be pleasant to think that problems with relations and friends as handled by Barbara Willard, Anne Pilgrim, Mary K Harris or Margaret Storey, could be as successfully smoothed out in real life. The approach of Emily Cheney Neville tended to be more realistic. A Philippa Pearce kept a firm grasp on reality in *A dog so small*, while John Rowe Townsend showed his awareness of the grimmer side of life in *Gumble's Yard* and its sequel *Widdershins Crescent*. Australian Reginald Ottley offered no easy solutions in *The Bates family*. It is wrong, as Kitty Barne has said, to offer a child false solutions. Even a child must surely query some of the idyllic dénouements offered in children's books of the 1960's: the providential materialisation of a forgotten aunt in *The hunt for Harry* by Rosemary Weir; the remarriage of an uncongenial father in *Fly-by-night* by K M Peyton; or the mothers arranging to char for the West Indians in *Ginger and number 10* by Prudence Andrew. *Beat of the city* by Australian H F Brinsmead particularly refrains from idyllic solutions, while Mrs E L Konigsburg closed the fantasy-like *Jennifer, Hecate, Macbeth and me,* with the rational solution of an ordinary little-girl friendship. John Rowe Townsend also offered no romantic conclusion to *Widdershins Crescent*, which ended with Kevin leaving school to become an errand boy instead of going on to grammar school.

The best problems offer children an intellectual challenge and clearly show all facets of a situation. In her article ' Social values in children's literature ' in *Library quarterly*, January 1967, Emily Cheney Neville wrote that she believed that the ' way a child learns to love and hate in his own family must have a great deal to do with how he acts when he confronts situations of anti-semitism, integration and similar critical social issues '. She wisely went on to advise that the author's aim is ' not to show the reader how to be a hero, but how hard it is to be a plain, decent human being '.

On these grounds, authors of family stories have a duty to ensure that their books contribute benevolently to the formation of a child's attitudes. But there was, on the other hand, some danger in the 1960's of this sense of duty being carried to excess, a situation deplored by Eleanor von Schweinitz in her article ' The new golden age ' in *Children's book news*, May-June, 1969, in which she expressed particular concern over the possibility of the purely imaginative and creative talents of writers for children being submerged by the fashion for didacticism.

74

chapter five

CONCLUSION

In a short book such as this, it is obviously only possible to scratch the surface of a quite large area of literature, and to reflect mainly personal views and judgments, though the preceding chapters have tried in brief to examine material still too new to have faced the searching test of time. Children's literature is a *genre* in which only a few outstanding books are likely to survive even so long as a decade. In the introduction to this book reference was made to a talk, *The development of the family story,* given in 1958. After writing the first four chapters of the present work, it has proved salutary to compare the conclusions reached then with those arrived at more than a decade later.

The basic defect of the family story is its transitory nature. By definition, it normally presents the family in a contemporaneous framework, which in the space of a few years can change radically, so as to render much of its literature dated or meaningless to a later generation of readers. It has already been stressed that, for his work to survive, the writer of the family story is wise to avoid references which are too superficially topical or current. The readable life of a good family story may be as much as twenty or thirty years, but this is unusual. Some of the examples used in the talk of 1958 are virtually forgotten today. It is equally certain that many of the books used for this study of the family story in the 1960's will be similarly neglected ten years hence.

Flaws in the traditional mould of the family story were all too apparent in 1958, and were in some cases a legacy from earlier writers: parents were conspicuous by their absence; characterisation of both children and adults was frequently minimal; sound material based on real life was sometimes spoiled in conjunction with impossible adventures; a strictly limited number of books was related to the real life of the majority of children; and, lastly, there was a noticeable lack of material in this category aimed at the teenager not yet mature enough for adult fiction.

The pattern of the family story over the last two hundred years suggests that it takes many decades for significant changes to evolve. Most of the conclusions of 1958 are valid at the end of the 1960's with only slight modifications: parents were dispensed with in about forty percent of the family stories of the 1960's, an alarming proportion of this number being disposed of in air or road accidents. If present, parents were often less shadowy figures than in the pre-1960 period, although, on investigation, their role tended to be played more within the home, and less in joint activities outside the confines of home, than would be expected in real life. In the handling of characterisation, perhaps the most penetrating changes in the last decade lie, on the one hand, in authors' creations of convincing adult characters, with faults and virtues, with feelings and attitudes, and with admitted difficulties to face, and, on the other hand, in their presentation of relationships between children and adults outside the family. These changes reflect the gradual alteration of social attitudes, from both the nineteenth century, when parents, though not always the other adults, were mainly presented as impeccable characters who could do no wrong, and from the 1930's, when parents tended in the main to be summarily dismissed from the stories.

Perhaps it is the reduction of the extended family of earlier generations to the immediate family of today which has caused increased involvement on the part of children with other adults outside the family, a trend most noticeably reflected in the family story of the 1960's, as was the maturity with which the characterisation of outside adults was handled by most authors. In some books, adults outside the family played more important roles than near relatives, and were often described more vividly and sympathetically than the hapless parents.

Apart from the consistently high mortality of parents, it could be said that there were healthy signs of growth in the area of adult presentation in the family story of the 1960's. In many instances adults emerged as more rounded characters than the children. In 1958, the sketchy presentation of child characters was deplored, and it is regrettable that this criticism can still be justified at the end of the 1960's. Another weakness is that the relationships between children were neglected by many writers of the 1960's, or else handled at a very rudimentary level. This has already been tentatively attributed to the age gap between child and writer, successfully bridged only by a few discerning authors.

In 1958, the present author spoke of ' good material spoiled by fantastic, unnecessary adventures ', and although this is still true, the pendulum is in some danger of swinging the other way; by the end of the 1960's, a common ground of criticism concerned the growing tendency for authors to instruct and moralise within the framework of the family story. By the end of the 1960's it could be said that realistic problems of varying magnitudes were being used by some authors wholly in lieu of fantasy.

In 1958, the teenager's needs were sadly neglected, a situation recognised by the end of the 1960's, but little nearer solution. During the 1950's, a rash of ' career ' novels attempted to fill the gap in material for young people too mature for junior fiction, but not ready for adult literature. The variety of family stories available for older girls increased marginally during the 1960's, and some publishers, notably Heinemann and Macmillan, introduced specific series for teenagers, but an uneasy situation persisted, with little hope of immediate solution. As the majority of these novels presented highly diluted versions of the lives and problems likely to face teenagers in real life, their value was to that extent questionable. Aidan Chambers studied aspects of the difficult problem of teenage reading in

77

The reluctant reader, and showed serious concern over the limitations of the material available.

In attempting to assess some of the patterns emerging at the end of the 1960's, it is relevant to remember the stricture of Roger Lancelyn Green, who, in *Tellers of tales,* correctly assessed the difficulties when he wrote that ' with most recent books we are too near to be able to judge properly: we cannot see the trees for the wood '. He suggested that in trying to gauge the value of current material, it is only possible to select potentially outstanding works and to accept the judgments of both critics and children.

From the family stories published during the 1960's it is possible to gain a more complete picture than before of the different nature of family relationships throughout the world: between siblings, between parents and children, and to a considerably reduced extent, between children and other relatives. The gradual erosion of the family unit was evident in many family stories, and in a reasonably representative sample taken from among those published in the 1960's, the following details emerged: thirty seven percent of the books examined had one or both parents missing; grandparents appeared in ten percent of the selected titles, but other relations were prominent mainly when parents were absent or dead. Books by at least two authors were unusual in their treatment of the family in the 1960's: Elfrida Vipont's *The pavilion,* published in 1969, is the fifth volume of the series started in 1948 with her distinguished book *The lark in the morn*; and Barbara Willard wrote two books concentrated on the ramifications of the Tower family. The books of both these authors centre almost exclusively on activities within the broader confines of the family, and have more affinity with family stories of an earlier period than the 1960's, in spite of their topical references.

In everyday life, one of the most definitive changes of the decade was the altered emphasis between home and school life. By the 1950's, the demise of the boarding school story for girls was generally accepted, although the boys' school story had faded out considerably earlier. In the 1960's there were signs of the development of stories which satisfactorily linked school and home, a combination which was the real life experience for the great majority of children. This mixture of home and school life could be traced in approximately forty four percent of the sample already mentioned. In another twenty percent of the sample, children in the stories attended boarding schools, although the action regularly occurred during a holiday period; while in the remaining thirty six percent, school of any kind was entirely in the background. Obviously, different samples of books might produce variations in results, but it does seem significant that there was still so marked a preoccupation with boarding school, where in reality only one percent of the UK's school population is involved.

In authors' treatment of everyday life, the material examined for the present book makes it clear that during the 1960's authors made a genuine, if not always successful attempt to cater for working class children's needs on a scale never previously attempted, though few of them dealt with the mean between affluence and poverty. Since the late 1940's, critics have persistently agitated for more material about working class children, with so much effect that it has not perhaps been realised to what extent the amount has increased since its virtual non-existence in the 1930's. In the sample mentioned, twenty four percent of the material had an upper middle class setting; thirty percent had a reasonably middle class setting; seven percent had a mixture of middle and working class, while in spite of an unclassifiable three percent, the remaining thirty six percent of the settings were definitely working class; a larger proportion than any of the other groups. It can be pointed out that the majority of real children are in this group, so that the picture given in the family story is somewhat distorted in comparison with reality, but far less so than it was thirty years ago. Ideally, all kinds of background deserve to be represented in the family story, to reflect a full picture of real life, and to give children from all walks of life the opportunity to recognise and identify, if they wish, with the characters in the books they read.

Whatever the faults of the family story of the 1960's, credit is at least due for the slow transformation which has taken place since the 1930's. During the last thirty years, the family story has had to adjust to tremendous social change. It must now show a corresponding awareness of the varied interests of children today, though individual authors write with their own aims in mind, so that any pattern discerned from the whole area of the family story is perhaps coincidental. But compared with the 1930 period, the 1960's generally showed more awareness of parents and adults, more concern over problems than over trivial adventures, more combinations of home and school life, a far wider variety of social backgrounds, and a more extensive range of children's interests, activities and hobbies.

Whatever criticisms can be levelled at British writers for their failures in the field of the family story, they are modest in comparison with the majority of children's books from Europe which were made available in translated editions; very few of these gave a representative picture of family life, or qualified as family stories in the accepted sense.

In 1958 it was difficult to forecast with any degree of accuracy the probable direction of the family story in the 1960's, and it would be equally invidious to be dogmatic about the ways in which it may develop in the 1970's. At the end of the 1960's there were some signs of increasing concern with morality, an indication of awareness on the part of some authors of the disadvantages of the permissive society, and this may indicate a new trend in subject treatment. It is also desirable that during the 1970's writers should emerge in greater numbers from an increasingly literate working class, and also from a better integrated immigrant community, to make their own contribution to the family story. The majority of writers of family stories in the 1960's failed adequately to reflect the real life and attitudes of the period. In the 1970's it seems likely that this pattern will persist. Some authors will doubtless continue to use traditional formulae, others will reflect the life of some vaguely imagined post-war period, while a perceptive few, it may be hoped, will succeed in capturing for young readers the true essence of their period.

SOURCES OF INFORMATION

Anonymous 'Class literature' *Times literary supplement* 19th May 1966 438-9.

Anonymous 'Eleanor Graham' *Junior bookshelf* 26(3) July 1962 101-2.

Anonymous 'Mary K Harris: the real world of school' *Times literary supplement* 5th December 1968 1379.

Anonymous 'Wanted a literature' *Times literary supplement* 23rd November 1956 ix.

Anonymous 'William Mayne: writer disordinary' *Times literary supplement* 24th November 1966 1080.

Gillian Avery *Mrs Ewing* (Bodley Head, 1961; NY, Walck, 1964).

Gillian Avery *Nineteenth century children: heroes and heroines of English children's stories 1780-1900* (Hodder & Stoughton, 1965).

Juliana Bayfield 'From Simon Black to Ash Road and beyond' *Bookbird* 6(4) December 1968 33-5.

Anthea Bell *E Nesbit* (Bodley Head, 1960; NY, Walck, 1964).

Edward Blishen 'William Mayne' *Use of English* 20(2) Winter 1968 99-103.

George Bott 'Arthur Ransome' *School librarian* 10(3) December 1960 203-10.

George Bott 'A little lower than the angels: a tribute to Arthur Ransome' *Junior bookshelf* 28(1) January 1964 15-21.

Joan E Cass *Literature and the young child* (Longmans, 1967).

Aidan Chambers *The reluctant reader* (Pergamon, 1969).

Berna Clark (editor) *Books for primary children* (School Library Association, 1969).

Eileen Colwell 'Kitty Barne: an appreciation' *Junior bookshelf* 25(4) October 1961 197-201.

Eileen Colwell and others (editors) *First choice: a basic booklist for children* (Library Association, 1968).

Marcus Crouch (editor) *Chosen for children: an account of the books which have been awarded the Library Association Carnegie Medal 1936-1965* (Library Association, 1967).

Marcus Crouch 'Dr Arthur Ransome, CBE' *Junior Bookshelf* 31(4) August 1967 219-20.

Marcus Crouch 'E Nesbit in Kent' *Junior Bookshelf* 19(1) January 1955 11-21.

Marcus Crouch *Treasure seekers and borrowers: children's books in Britain 1900-1960* (Library Association, 1962).

F J Harvey Darton *Children's books in England: five centuries of social life* second edition (Cambridge University Press, 1958).

Brian Doyle (editor) *The who's who of children's literature* (Hugh Evelyn, 1968).

Alec Ellis *A history of children's reading and literature* (Pergamon, 1968).

Alec Ellis *How to find out about children's literature* second edition (Pergamon, 1968).

Alec and Anne Ellis 'The family story as a reflection of reality' *Junior bookshelf* 31(5) October 1967 303-7.

Anne Ellis 'The family in fiction' *School librarian* 16(3) December 1968 281-4.

Anne Ellis 'To survive or not to survive?' *Library review* 21(6) Summer 1968 290-2.

Elizabeth Enright 'Realism in children's literature' *The Horn book magazine* 43(2) April 1967 165-70.

Frank Eyre *Twentieth century children's books* (Longmans, 1952).

Margery Fisher *Intent upon reading: a critical appraisal of modern fiction for children* second edition (Brockhampton, 1964).

Margery Fisher 'Patricia Wrightson' *School librarian* 17(1) March 1969 22-6.

Boris Ford (editor) *Young writers, young readers: an anthology of children's reading and writing* second edition (Hutchinson, 1963).

H Fotheringham 'The art of William Mayne' *Junior bookshelf* 23(4) October 1959 185-9.

Eleanor Graham 'The Carnegie medal and its winners' *Junior bookshelf* 8(3) July 1944 59-65.

Roger Lancelyn Green 'E Nesbit: treasure seeker' *Junior bookshelf* 22(4) October 1958 175-85.

Roger Lancelyn Green *Mrs Molesworth* (Bodley Head, 1961; NY, Walck, 1964).

Roger Lancelyn Green *Tellers of tales: children's books and their authors from 1800 to 1968* fifth edition (Kaye & Ward, 1969, NY, Watts, 1969).

James Guthrie 'Realism and escapism in children's literature' *Junior bookshelf* 22(1) January 1958 15-18.

Paul Hazard *Books, children and men;* translated by Marguerite Mitchell (Boston, Horn Book Inc, 1944; Flammarion, 1932).

Nat Hentoff 'Getting inside *Jazz country*' *The Horn book magazine* 42(5) October 1966 528-32.

Janet A Hill 'A minority view' *Children's book news* 2(3) May-June 1967 109-12.

Lee Bennett Hopkins 'Negro life in current American children's literature' *Bookbird* 6(1) March 1968 12-16.

Bettina Hürlimann *Three centuries of children's books in Europe;* translated by Brian W Alderson (Oxford University Press, 1967; Zurich, Atlantis Verlag, 1959).

Lee Kingman (editor) *Newbery and Caldecott medal books 1956-1965* (Boston, Horn Book Inc, 1965).

Marghanita Laski (editor) *Victorian tales for girls* (Pilot Press, 1947).

Naomi Lewis (editor) *The best children's books of 1963* (Hamish Hamilton, 1964).

Naomi Lewis (editor) *The best children's books of 1964* (Hamish Hamilton, 1965).

Naomi Lewis (editor) *The best children's books of 1965* (Hamish Hamilton, 1966).

Naomi Lewis (editor) *The best children's books of 1966* (Hamish Hamilton, 1967).

Naomi Lewis (editor) *The best children's books of 1967* (Hamish Hamilton, 1969).

Library Association, Youth Libraries Section *Books for young people* Groups 1-3 (Library Association, 1952-60).

Kathleen Lines (editor) *Four to fourteen: a library of books for children* second edition (Cambridge University Press, 1956).

Derek Lomas 'Arthur Ransome: a birthday appreciation' *Junior bookshelf* 28(1) January 1964 27-9.

Margaret Meek *Geoffrey Trease* (Bodley Head, 1960; NY, Walck, 1964).

Bertha Mahony Miller and Elinor Whitney Field (editors) *Newbery medal books 1922-1955* (Boston, Horn Book Inc, 1955).

Percival H Muir *English children's books 1600 to 1900* (Batsford, 1954; NY, Praeger, 1954).

National Book League *British children's books* second edition (National Book League, 1967).

National Book League *School library fiction: children and adults* (National Book League, 1966).

Emily Cheney Neville 'Out where the real people are' *The Horn book magazine* 40(4) August 1964 400-4.

Emily Cheney Neville 'Social values in children's literature' *Library quarterly* 37(1) January 1967 46-52.

Doreen Norman 'The books of Prudence Andrew' *Books for your children* 4(1) October 1968 4-5.

Ann Philippa Pearce 'Writing a book' *The Horn book magazine* 43(3) June 1967 317-22.

Hugh Shelley *Arthur Ransome* (Bodley Head, 1960; NY, Walck, 1964).

Noel Streatfeild 'The Nesbit influence' *Junior bookshelf* 22(4) October 1958 187-93.

Noel Streatfeild 'Oswald Bastable' *The Horn book magazine* 34(5) October 1958 366-72.

Sunday Times *The one hundred best books for children* (Sunday Times, 1958).

University College of Swansea, Faculty of Education Centre *Prize winning books for children* (University College of Swansea, 1965).

J K G Taylor ' The social background of children's fiction ' *School librarian* 10(3) December 1962 231-43.

Mary F Thwaite (editor) *Children's books of this century: a first list of books covering the years 1899-1956* (Library Association, 1958).

Mary F Thwaite *From primer to pleasure: an introduction to the history of children's books in England from the invention of printing to 1900* (Library Association, 1963).

Claire Tomalin ' Goodbye hockey-sticks ' *The observer* 8th December 1968 30.

John Rowe Townsend ' Didacticism in modern dress ' *The Horn book magazine* 43(2) April 1967 159-64.

John Rowe Townsend ' The present state of English children's literature ' *Wilson library bulletin* 43(2) October 1968 126-33.

John Rowe Townsend *Written for children: an outline of children's literature* (Garnet Miller, 1965).

Geoffrey Trease *Tales out of school* second edition (Heinemann, 1964).

Philip Turner ' Philip Turner ' *Junior bookshelf* 30(3) June 1966 160-2.

Ruth Hill Viguers *Margin for surprise: about books, children, and libraries* (Constable Young Books, 1966; Boston, Little, Brown, 1964).

Eleanor von Schweinitz ' The new golden age ' *Children's book news* 4(3) May-June 1969 117-9.

Dorothy Neal White *About books for children* (Oxford University Press, 1949; Wellington, New Zealand Council for Educational Research, 1946).

Barbara Ker Wilson *Noel Streatfeild* (Bodley Head, 1961; NY, Walck, 1964).

Eva von Zweigbergk 'Aims and ideals reflected in children's books ' *Bookbird* 6(3) September 1968 3-14.

FAMILY STORIES OF THE 1960's

All titles in this list are mentioned in the text except those marked with an asterisk.

Mabel Esther Allan *Tansy of Tring Street;* illustrated by Sally Holliday (Heinemann, 1960).

Eric Allen *The latchkey children;* illustrated by Charles Keeping (Oxford University Press, 1963).

Prudence Andrew *Ginger and number 10;* illustrated by Charles Mozley (Lutterworth, 1964).

Ruth M Arthur *Dragon summer;* illustrated by Margery Gill (Hutchinson, 1962).

Ruth M Arthur *Portrait of Margarita;* illustrated by Margery Gill (Gollancz, 1968).

Ruth M Arthur *Requiem for a princess;* illustrated by Margery Gill (Gollancz, 1967).

Ruth M Arthur *The whistling boy;* illustrated by Margery Gill (Gollancz, 1969).*

Honor Arundel *Emma's island* (Hamish Hamilton, 1968).

Honor Arundel *Green Street;* illustrated by Eileen Armitage (Hamish Hamilton, 1966).

Honor Arundel *The high house;* illustrated by Eileen Armitage (Hamish Hamilton, 1966).

Honor Arundel *The two sisters* (Heinemann, Pyramid Books, 1968).

Margaret J Baker *Castaway Christmas;* illustrated by Richard Kennedy (Methuen, 1963).

Margaret J Baker *Cut off from crumpets;* illustrated by Richard Kennedy (Methuen, 1964).

Anne Barrett *Midway;* illustrated by Margery Gill (Collins, 1967).

Nina Bawden *The secret passage* (Gollancz, 1963).*

George Beardmore *Islands of strangers;* illustrated by Richard Kennedy (Macdonald, 1968).

Hesba Fay Brinsmead *Beat of the city;* illustrated by William Papas (Oxford University Press, 1966).

Hesba Fay Brinsmead *Pastures of the blue crane;* illustrated by Annette Macarthur-Onslow (Oxford University Press, 1964).

Hesba Fay Brinsmead *A sapphire for September;* illustrated by Victor Ambrus (Oxford University Press, 1967).*

Robert Burch *Skinny;* illustrated by Ian Ribbons (Methuen, 1965; NY, Viking Press, 1964).

Hester Burton *The great gale;* illustrated by Joan Kiddell-Monroe (Oxford University Press, 1960).

Aidan Chambers *Marle* (Heinemann, Pyramid Books, 1968).

Ruth Forbes Chandler *Ladder to the sky;* illustrated by Harper Johnson (Abelard-Schuman, 1965; NY, Abelard-Schuman, 1959).

Jill Chaney *Half a candle* (Dobson, 1968).*

Hugo Charteris *Clunie;* illustrated by Victor Ambrus (Heinemann, 1963).*

Hugo Charteris *Staying with Aunt Rozzie;* illustrated by Eric Thomas (Heinemann, 1964).*

Nan Chauncy *The lighthouse keeper's son;* illustrated by Victor Ambrus (Oxford University Press, 1969).*

Nan Chauncy *Lizzie Lights;* illustrated by Judith White (Oxford University Press, 1968).

Dorothy Clewes *A boy like Walt* (Collins, 1967).*

Dorothy Clewes *Guide dog* (Hamish Hamilton, 1965).

Mary Cockett *Rolling on;* illustrated by Shirley Hughes (Methuen, 1960).*

Catherine Cookson *Matty Doolin;* illustrated by Margery Gill (Macdonald, 1965).*

Margaret Dunnett *The people next door;* illustrated by Maurice Bartlett (Andre Deutsch, 1965).*

Maribel Edwin *Bilberry summer;* illustrated by Victor Ambrus (Collins, 1965).*

Maribel Edwin *The snowbound bus;* illustrated by Margery Gill (Nelson, 1960).

Eleanor Estes *Ginger Pye;* illustrated by Margery Gill (Bodley Head, 1961; NY, Harcourt, 1951).

Annabel Farjeon *Maria Lupin;* illustrated by James Hunt (Abelard-Schuman, 1967).

Penelope Farmer *The magic stone;* illustrated by John Kaufmann (Chatto & Windus, 1964).

Antonia Forest *Peter's room* (Faber, 1961).

Antonia Forrest *The ready-made family* (Faber, 1967).*

Antonia Forest *The Thursday kidnapping* (Faber, 1963).

Paula Fox *How many miles to Babylon?;* illustrated by Paul Giovanopoulos (Macmillan, 1968; NY, D White, 1967).

Babbis Friis *Kersti;* translated by Lise Sømme McKinnon (Hart-Davis, 1966; Oslo, Damm, 1962).

Frederick Grice *A Severnside story;* illustrated by William Papas (Oxford University Press, 1964).

Maria Gripe *Pappa Pellerin's daughter;* translated by Kersti French; illustrated by Harold Gripe (Chatto & Windus, 1966; Stockholm, Bonnier, 1963).

Mary Kathleen Harris *The bus girls;* illustrated by Eileen Green (Faber, 1965).

Mary Kathleen Harris *Jessica on her own;* illustrated by Alison Prince (Faber, 1968).

Mary Kathleen Harris *Penny's way;* illustrated by Sheila Rose (Faber, 1963).

Mary Kathleen Harris *Seraphina;* illustrated by Sheila Rose (Faber, 1960).

Nat Hentoff *Jazz country* (Hart-Davis, 1966; NY, Harper & Row, 1965).

88

E W Hildick *Meet Lemon Kelly;* illustrated by Margery Gill (Cape, 1963).

E W Hildick *The questers;* illustrated by Richard Rose (Brockhampton, 1966).

Charlotte Hough *The owl in the barn;* illustrated by the author (Faber, 1964).

Delia Huddy *No place like Tricketts Green;* illustrated by Colin Wheeler (Longmans Young Books, 1968).*

Irene Hunt *Up a road slowly* (Macdonald, 1967; Chicago, Follett, 1966).*

Nan Inger *Katrin;* translated by Joan Tate (Hamish Hamilton, 1967; Stockholm, Rabén & Sjögren, 1966).

Josephine Kamm *No strangers here* (Constable Young Books, 1968).

Josephine Kamm *Out of step;* illustrated by Jillian Willett (Brockhampton, 1962).

Elaine L Konigsburg *From the mixed-up files of Mrs Basil E Frankweiler;* illustrated by the author (Macmillan, 1969; NY, Athenaeum, 1968).

Elaine L Konigsburg *Jenifer, Hecate, Macbeth and me;* illustrated by the author (Macmillan, 1968; NY, Athenaeum, 1967).

Joseph Krumgold *Onion John;* illustrated by Symeon Shimin (Lutterworth, 1964; NY, Thomas Y Crowell, 1959).

Lois Lamplugh *The linhay on Hunter's Hill;* illustrated by Laszlo Acs (Andre Deutsch, 1966).

Lois Lamplugh *The sixpenny runner;* illustrated by William Stobbs (Cape, 1960).*

Angela Latini *Za the truffle boy;* translated by Archibald Colquhoun; illustrated by Pino Dell'Orco (University of London Press, 1960; Turin, Paravia, 1955).

Jean Little *Mine for keeps;* illustrated by Lewis Parker (Dent, 1964; Boston, Little, Brown, 1962).*

A Rutgers van der Loeff *Rossie;* translated by Edward Fitzgerald (University of London Press, 1964; Amsterdam, Ploegsma, 1963).

Alice Low *Kallie's corner;* illustrated by David Stone Martin (Pantheon Books, 1966).*

Alice Lunt *Eileen of Redstone Farm;* illustrated by Maureen Eckersley (Dent, 1964).

Alice Lunt *Secret stepmother: a story for girls;* illustrated by D G Valentine (Dent, 1964).*

Reginald Maddock *The Pit;* illustrated by Douglas Hall (Collins, 1966).*

M-J Malavié *The canary tree;* translated by Thelma Niklaus (Bodley Head, 1969; Paris, Societé Nouvelle des Editions G P, 1966).*

William Mayne *The battlefield;* illustrated by Mary Russon (Hamish Hamilton, 1967).*

William Mayne *The changeling;* illustrated by Victor Ambrus (Oxford University Press, 1961).

William Mayne *Earthfasts* (Hamish Hamilton, 1966).

William Mayne *A parcel of trees;* illustrated by Margery Gill (Hamish Hamilton, 1963).

William Mayne *The rolling season;* illustrated by Christopher Brooker (Oxford University Press, 1960).

William Mayne *Sand;* illustrated by Margery Gill (Hamish Hamilton, 1964).

William Mayne *Summer visitors;* illustrated by William Stobbs (Oxford University Press, 1961).

Emily Cheney Neville *Berries Goodman* (NY, Harper & Row, 1965).

Emily Cheney Neville *It's like this, cat;* illustrated by Emil Weiss (NY, Harper & Row, 1963).

Emily Cheney Neville *The Seventeenth Street gang;* illustrated by Emily McCully (NY, Harper & Row, 1966).

Peter Henry Nortje *The dark waters;* illustrated by William Papas (Oxford University Press, 1965; Cape Town, Tafelberg-Uitgeivers (Edms) Bpk, 1964).*

Peter Henry Nortje *Wild goose summer;* illustrated by William Papas (Oxford University Press, 1964; Cape Town, Tafelberg-Uitgeivers (Edms) Bpk, 1959).

Reginald Ottley *The Bates family* (Collins, 1969).

Margaret Paice *The Bensens;* illustrated by the author (Collins, 1968).*

C Everard Palmer *The cloud with the silver lining;* illustrated by Laszlo Acs (Andre Deutsch, 1966).

Richard Parker *The boy who wasn't lonely;* illustrated by Prudence Seward (Brockhampton, 1964).

Richard Parker *Private beach;* illustrated by Victor Ambrus (Harrap, 1964).

Richard Parker *Second-hand family;* illustrated by Gareth Floyd (Brockhampton, 1965).

Ann Philippa Pearce *A dog so small;* illustrated by Antony Maitland (Constable, 1962).

K M Peyton *Fly-by-night;* illustrated by the author (Oxford University Press, 1968).

K M Peyton *The plan for Birdsmarsh;* illustrated by Victor Ambrus (Oxford University Press, 1965).

Joan Phipson *The family conspiracy;* illustrated by Margaret Horder (Constable, 1962; Angus & Robertson, 1962).

Joan Phipson *Peter and Butch* (Longmans Young Books, 1969).*

Anne Pilgrim *Selina's new family;* illustrated by Graham Byfield (Abelard-Schuman, 1967).

Sheena Porter *The bronze chrysanthemum;* illustrated by Shirley Hughes (Oxford University Press, 1961).

Sheena Porter *Deerfold;* illustrated by Victor Ambrus (Oxford University Press, 1966).

Sheena Porter *Hills and hollows;* illustrated by Victor Ambrus (Oxford University Press, 1962).

Sheena Porter *Jacob's ladder;* illustrated by Victor Ambrus (Oxford University Press, 1963).*

Sheena Porter *Nordy Bank;* illustrated by Annette Macarthur-Onslow (Oxford University Press, 1964).

Sheena Porter *The scapegoat;* illustrated by Doreen Roberts (Oxford University Press, 1968).

Renée Reggiani *The adventures of five children and a dog;* translated by Antonia Nevill; illustrated by Geraldine Spence (Collins, 1963; Bologna, Capelli, 1960).

Renée Reggiani *The sun train;* translated by Patrick Creagh; (Harrap, 1966; Milan, A Garzanti, 1962).*

Veronica Robinson *David in silence;* illustrated by Victor Ambrus (Andre Deutsch, 1965).

Andrew Salkey *Drought;* illustrated by William Papas (Oxford University Press, 1966).

Andrew Salkey *Hurricane;* illustrated by William Papas (Oxford University Press, 1964).

Sylvia Sherry *Frog in a coconut shell* (Cape, 1968).*

Sylvia Sherry *A pair of Jesus-boots* (Cape, 1969).

Barbara Sleigh *No one must know;* illustrated by Jillian Willett (Collins, 1962).

Emma Smith *Out of hand;* illustrated by Antony Maitland (Macmillan, 1963).*

Vian Smith *The Lord Mayor's show* (Longmans Young Books, 1968).

Virginia Sorensen *Miracles on Maple Hill;* illustrated by Beth and Joe Krush (Brockhampton, 1967; NY, Harcourt, 1956).

Ivan Southall *Ash Road;* illustrated by Clem Seale (Angus & Robertson, 1966).

Ivan Southall *Finn's Folly* (Angus & Robertson, 1969).

Ivan Southall *Hills End* (Angus & Robertson, 1962).

Ivan Southall *To the wild sky;* illustrated by Jennifer Tuckwell (Angus & Robertson, 1967).

Eleanor Spence *The green laurel;* illustrated by Geraldine Spence (Oxford University Press, 1963).

Eleanor Spence *Patterson's Track;* illustrated by Alison Forbes (Oxford University Press, 1963; Melbourne, Oxford University Press, 1958).

Eleanor Spence *The year of the currawong;* illustrated by Gareth Floyd (Oxford University Press, 1965).

Margaret Storey *Kate and the family tree;* illustrated by Shirley Hughes (Bodley Head, 1965).*

Margaret Storey *Pauline* (Faber, 1965).

Noel Streatfeild *Apple bough;* illustrated by Margery Gill (Collins, 1962).*

Noel Streatfeild *The children on the top floor;* illustrated by Jillian Willett (Collins, 1964).

Noel Streatfeild *The growing summer;* illustrated by Edward Ardizzone (Collins, 1966).

Elizabeth Stucley *Magnolia Buildings;* illustrated by Dick Hart (Bodley Head, 1960).

Marie Thøger *Shanta;* translated from the Danish by Eileen Amos (University of London Press, 1966; Copenhagen, Gyldendal, 1961).

John Rowe Townsend *Gumble's Yard;* illustrated by Dick Hart (Hutchinson, 1961).

John Rowe Townsend *The Hallersage sound* (Hutchinson, 1966).

John Rowe Townsend *Hell's Edge* (Hutchinson, 1963).

John Rowe Townsend *The intruder;* illustrated by Graham Humphreys (Oxford University Press, 1969).*

John Rowe Townsend *Pirate's island;* illustrated by Douglas Hall (Oxford University Press, 1968).

John Rowe Townsend *Widdershins Crescent* (Hutchinson, 1965).

Mary Treadgold *The winter princess;* illustrated by Pearl Falconer (Brockhampton, 1962).

Geoffrey Trease *Change at Maythorn;* illustrated by Robert Hodgson (Heinemann, 1962).*

Geoffrey Trease *The Maythorn story;* illustrated by Robert Hodgson (Heinemann, 1960).

Philip Turner *Colonel Sheperton's clock;* illustrated by Philip Gough (Oxford University Press, 1964).

Philip Turner *The Grange at High Force;* illustrated by William Papas (Oxford University Press, 1965).

Philip Turner *Sea peril;* illustrated by Ian Ribbons (Oxford University Press, 1966).

Philip Turner *War on the Darnel*; illustrated by Doreen Roberts (Oxford University Press, 1969).*

Yoshiko Uchida *In-between Miya;* illustrated by Susan Bennett (Angus & Robertson, 1968; NY, Scribner, 1967).

Elfrida Vipont *Flowering spring;* illustrated by Shirley Hughes (Oxford University Press, 1960).

Elfrida Vipont *The pavilion;* illustrated by Prudence Seward (Oxford University Press, 1969).

Priscilla Warner *The Paradise summer;* illustrated by Prudence Seward (Collins, 1963).

Jenifer Wayne *Clemence and Ginger;* illustrated by Patricia Humphreys (Heinemann, 1960).

Jenifer Wayne *The ghost next door;* illustrated by Margaret Palmer (Heinemann, 1965).*

Jenifer Wayne *Merry by name;* illustrated by Margaret Palmer (Heinemann, 1964).*

Jenifer Wayne *The night the rain came in;* illustrated by Dodie Masterman (Heinemann, 1963).*

Jenifer Wayne *Ollie;* illustrated by Margaret Palmer (Heinemann, 1969).

Rosemary Weir *The hunt for Harry* (Parrish, 1960).

Rosemary Weir *The real game;* illustrated by Aedwin Darroll (Brockhampton, 1965).

Rosemary Weir *Soap-box Derby;* illustrated by Biro (Brockhampton, 1962).*

Ester Wier *The loner;* illustrated by Antony Maitland (Constable Young Books, 1966; NY, McKay, 1963).*

Ester Wier *The wind chasers;* illustrated by A R Whitear (Constable Young Books, 1968; NY, McKay, 1967).*

Barbara Willard *The battle of Wednesday week;* illustrated by Douglas Hall (Constable Young Books, 1963).

Barbara Willard *Charity at Home;* illustrated by Mary Rose Hardy (Constable Young Books, 1965).

Barbara Willard *Duck on a pond;* illustrated by Mary Rose Hardy (Constable Young Books, 1962).

Barbara Willard *Eight for a secret;* illustrated by Lewis Hart (Constable Young Books, 1960).*

Barbara Willard *The family Tower* (Longmans Young Books, 1968).

Barbara Willard *Three and one to carry;* illustrated by Douglas Hall (Constable Young Books, 1964).

Barbara Willard *The toppling Towers* (Longmans Young Books, 1969).

Robina Beckles Willson *Pineapple Palace;* illustrated by Victor Ambrus (Hart-Davis, 1964).

Robina Beckles Willson *A seraph in a box;* illustrated by Victor Ambrus (Hart-Davis, 1963).*

Patricia Wrightson *The feather star;* illustrated by Noela Young (Hutchinson, 1962).*

Patricia Wrightson *I own the racecourse!;* illustrated by Margaret Horder (Hutchinson, 1968).

Accidents 18, 33, 67, 76

Acting 12, 51, 54

Actresses 28, 64

Adjustment 25, 32, 34, 71

Adoption 34, 59, 66, 67, 71

Adults 9, 17, 18, 19, 21, 24, 28, 30, 33, 34, 35, 36, 37, 38, 39, 47, 48, 54, 59, 60, 61, 65, 67, 69, 72, 76, 77, 80, *See also* Aunts and other relatives; Actresses and other occupations

Adventures 11, 12, 13, 34, 37, 76, 77, 80

Adventures of five children and a dog, The 14, 34, 54

Adventures of Herr Baby, The 10

Adventures of Tom Sawyer, The 18

Alcott, Louisa M 10, 17, 53

Alderson, Brian 11

Alice, Thomas and Jane 26

Allan, Mabel Esther 73

Allen, Eric 23, 43, 63, 66, 70

Ambivalence 29, 58

Amputations 32, 69

Andrew, Prudence 22, 44, 59, 65, 68, 74

Animals 55, 72, 73 *See also* Pets and Individual animals

Anti-Semitism 61, 71, 74

Archeology 50, 51, 73

Arnold, Matthew 52

Art 22, 34

Arthur, Ruth M 16, 18, 30, 33, 53, 60, 65, 66, 67, 71

Arundel, Honor 18, 24, 33, 34, 39, 44, 50, 53, 60, 69, 70

Ash Road 38, 60, 69

Atkinson, M E 23, 62, 73

Attitudes 13, 15, 16, 18, 22, 23, 24, 25, 26, 27, 28, 31, 59, 63, 70, 74, 76, 80

August adventure 73

Aunts 18, 32, 33, 36, 46, 48, 64, 71, 74

Austen, Jane 52

Australia 40, 44, 60

Authors 9, 10, 12, 14, 15, 16, 17, 20, 21, 22, 23, 24, 25, 28, 29, 33, 34, 36, 37, 38, 39, 40, 41, 42, 43, 44, 45, 49, 50, 51, 52, 53, 54, 55, 56, 57, 59, 60, 61, 62, 63, 64, 66, 68, 69, 70, 71, 72, 73, 74, 75, 76, 77, 78, 79, 80 *See also* Individual authors and titles

Autistic children *See* Children, Autistic

Automobile Association 56
Autumn term 49
Avery, Gillian 57

Babies 14, 23, 43, 59
Baboons 49
Baby sitting 45
Bach, Johann Sebastian 53
Backgrounds 17, 23, 34, 35, 37, 38, 39, 41, 55, 79, 80 *See also* Family stories: Middle class background etc.
Backwardness 68
Bagnold, Enid 26
Baker, Margaret J 19, 23, 33, 45, 48, 54, 55, 60, 65, 70
Ballet 51
Bandmasters 34, 54
Bands 34, 47, 53, 54
' Bank Holidays ' 47
Barne, Kitty 23, 31, 53, 62, 74
Barrett, Anne 20, 24, 26, 28, 29, 31, 54, 60, 64
Baseball 50
Bates family, The 55, 74
Bathrooms 22
Battle of Wednesday week, The 17
Beardmore, George 69
Beat of the city 22, 30, 53, 59, 67, 74
Beatles, The 53, 56
Beethoven, Ludvig van 53
Berg, Leila 40
Berries Goodman 60, 71
Best children's books of 1966, The 59
Better to arrive 24
Beyond the jungle 70
Bible, The 31
Bird watching 51
Birds 73
Birth 24
Birthdays 45, 46
Blindness 67
Blyton, Enid 13
Boarding school *See* Schools, Boarding
Bodley Head Monographs 22, 39
Bonzon, Paul Jacques 14
Bookbird 16
Books 12, 16, 36, 38, 39, 40, 41, 47, 51, 52, 54, 56, 79
Books, children and men 38
' Bouncers ' 67
Boy and the donkey, The 68
Boy at the window, The 67

Boy friends 70
Boy who wasn't lonely, The 32, 66
Boys 17, 18, 19, 22, 25, 32, 33, 34, 35, 38, 48, 49, 51, 62, 66, 67, 68, 70, 73, 74, 78 *See also* Brothers, Grandsons, Sons
Brahms, Johannes 53
Brinsmead, H F 14, 19, 22, 23, 30, 32, 45, 48, 53, 59, 60, 67, 69, 71, 73, 74
Brisley, Joyce Lankester 11
Britain 11, 41, 42, 44, 45, 55, 56, 66
British Broadcasting Corporation 56
British Guiana 66
Brontës, The 52
Bronze chrysanthemum, The 46
Brothers 14, 18, 20, 21, 22, 28, 29, 31, 32, 33, 40, 72
Brown, Frances Litt 57
Brown, Pamela 54
Builders 22
Burch, Robert 14, 57, 68
Burnett, *Mrs* Frances Hodgson 11, 40
Burton, Hester 57, 60, 62
Bus conductors 66
Bus drivers 22
Bus girls, The 19, 24, 26, 42, 72
Bush fires 60
Business 23

Cafés 47
Camping 12, 38, 48, 50
' Career ' novels 77
Careers 22, 23, 24, 32, 53, 59
Caretakers 22
Carnegie Medal 62
Carpenters 25
Carrots 10
Cars 51
Carved lions, The 10, 12
Cass, Joan E 17, 58
Castaway Christmas 19, 23, 45, 54, 60
Castle Blair 10
Cats 55, 68, 73
Chambers, Aidan 32, 53, 77
Chandler, Ruth Forbes 22, 24, 27, 29, 45, 60, 65, 72
Changeling, The 48, 73
Characterisation 23, 33, 53, 76, 77
Charity at home 30, 34, 45, 46, 47
Charlesworth, Mary Louisa 10
Chauncy, Nan 14, 66
Cheshire 44

Children 9, 10, 11, 12, 13, 14, 15, 16, 17, 18, 19, 20, 21, 22, 23, 24, 25, 26, 27, 28, 29, 30, 33, 34, 35, 36, 37, 38, 39, 40, 41, 42, 43, 44, 45, 46, 47, 48, 49, 50, 51, 52, 53, 54, 55, 58, 59, 60, 61, 62, 63, 64, 65, 66, 67, 68, 70, 72, 73, 74, 76, 77, 78, 79, 80 *See also* Boys, Brothers, Daughters, Friends, Friendship, Girls, Siblings, Sisters, Sons, Teenagers

Children, Autistic 67, 71

Children, Disabled 59, 63, 67

Children, Handicapped 63, 67 *See also* Blindness, Deafness, Mongols

Children, Lost 61, 71, 72

Children, Only 18, 30, 31, 32

Children of Primrose Lane, The 62

Children of the house, The 19, 24

Children on the top floor, The 16, 23, 46

Children who lived in a barn, The 17

Children's book news 15, 74

Children's books in England 9

Children's literature 15, 39, 46, 49, 75

Chorister's cake 53

Christmas 45, 46, 47

Cinema 12, 45

Cities 32, 44 *See also* Edinburgh, London, New York

Clarinets 53

Class 15, 19, 39, 41

Classes, Middle 12, 13, 15, 19, 22, 26, 40

Classes, Upper middle 16, 39, 49

Classes, Working 12, 13, 39, 62, 79, 80

Clemence and Ginger 26, 40, 64

Clergy 19, 22, 25, 34

Clewes, Dorothy 45, 53, 67

Cloud with the silver lining, The 32, 55, 69

Clubs 50

Colonel Sheperton's clock 41, 67

Colour *See* Racial issues

Comics 56

Composers 53, 54

Composing 54

Comprehensive schools *See* Schools, Comprehensive

Concerts 45, 53

Conducting 54

Contractors 22

Cookery 42

Coolidge, Susan 11, 17

Coronation Street 56

Cosmetics 26

Country 23, 32, 44, 48

Cousins 32, 33, 36, 46, 71

Crashes 18, 27, 30, 33

Creeds 15

Cricket 50

Crises 20, 27, 33, 60, 66

Criteria 15

Critical approach to children's literature, A 69

Critics 22, 31, 38, 46, 60, 78, 79

Crompton, Frances 10, 19

Cuckoo clock, The 10

Cummins, Maria Susanna 11, 52

Current issues 20, 55, 56, 59, 63, 65, 73, 74, 78

Customs 41, 45

Cut off from Crumpets 33, 48, 60, 65, 70

Daisy chain, The 10

Darton, F J Harvey 9

Daughters 25, 26, 27, 28, 30, 36, 64, 65, 71

David in silence 67

Day, Thomas 9, 17

De Selincourt, Aubrey 62

Deafness 67

Death 9, 16, 17, 18, 23, 24, 30, 32, 33, 36, 59, 63, 67, 69, 71, 77, 78

Deerfold 30, 34, 42, 72

Delinquency 62

Dickens, Charles 52

Didacticism 9, 13, 38, 40, 56, 57, 59, 63, 74

Dimbleby, Richard 56

Disabled children *See* **Children, Disabled**

Divorce 18, 59, 63, 64, 65

Doctors 19, 25

Dog so small, A 29, 31, 32, 46, 47, 54, 55, 73, 74

Dogs 27, 33, 43, 46, 54, 55, 73, 74

Dolphin crossing, The 62

Doyle, Brian 13

Dragon summer 65

Draughtsmen 22

Drought 48, 50, 60

Droughts 60

Drugs *See* Heroin

Duck on a pond 72, 73
Dustmen 71

Early lessons 9
Earthfasts 13, 25
Edgeworth, Maria 9, 15, 17
Edinburgh 33, 44
Education 19, 24, 26, 39, 59
Education acts 12
Edwin, Maribel 24, 50, 60
Eight cousins 10
Eileen of Redstone Farm 45, 68
Elder, Josephine 61
Electricians 24
Elidor 13, 40, 44
Ellis, Anne 20
Elsie Dinsmore books 11
Emergencies *See* Crises
Emma's island 44, 70
Employment 62
End of term 65
Engine drivers 22
England 38, 40, 66, *See also* Cheshire, Liverpool, London, Manchester, Oxford, Shropshire, Wiltshire, Yorkshire
Enright, Elizabeth 13, 14, 18, 47, 72
Estes, Eleanor 13, 14, 18, 43
Europe 44
Everyday life 16, 20, 23, 30, 35, 37, 38, 39, 40, 41, 42, 43, 45, 49, 50, 51, 55, 56, 61, 78, 79
Ewing, *Mrs* Juliana Horatia 9, 10
Exhibitions 45
Extended family *See* Family, Extended
Eyre, Frank 16, 39

Factories 22
Fairfax-Lucy, Brian 19, 24
Falcons 55
Family conspiracy, The 27
Family, Extended 18, 31, 34, 36, 77, 78
Family from One End Street, The 12, 13, 47, 62
Family stories: 18th century 9, 12, 15, 17, 34
Family stories: 19th century 9, 10, 11, 12, 15, 16, 17, 20, 22, 34, 40, 41
Family stories: early 20th century 11, 15, 24, 40

Family stories: 1930's 12, 13, 17, 23, 26, 31, 35, 36, 37, 38, 39, 40, 43, 45, 47, 48, 49, 52, 53, 54, 55, 56, 60, 61, 62, 73, 76, 79, 80
Family stories: 1940's 13, 17, 28, 31, 47, 49, 51, 53, 54, 56, 60, 61, 62, 72, 78
Family stories: 1950's 13, 14, 17, 25, 28, 35, 39, 42, 43, 45, 49, 50, 51, 52, 53, 54, 55, 60, 61, 62, 65, 68, 73, 77, 78
Family stories: 1960's 11, 13, 14, 15, 16, 17, 18, 19, 20, 21, 22, 23, 24, 25, 26, 27, 28, 29, 30, 31, 32, 33, 34, 35, ‘ 36, 37, 38, 39, 40, 41, 42, 43, 44, 45, 46, 47, 48, 49, 50, 51, 52, 53, 54, 55, 56, 57, 59, 60, 61, 62, 63, 64, 65, 66, 67, 68, 69, 70, 71, 72, 73, 74, 76, 77, 78, 79, 80
Family stories: 1970's 51, 52, 57, 80
Family stories: Australia 14, 19, 22, 25, 27, 30, 32, 37, 38, 45, 48, 49, 50, 53, 54, 55, 59, 60, 62, 64, 65, 66, 67, 69, 71, 72, 73, 74
Family stories: Britain 9, 10, 11, 12, 13, 15, 16, 17, 18, 19, 20, 21, 22, 23, 24, 25, 26, 27, 28, 29, 30, 31, 32, 33, 34, 35, 36, 37, 38, 39, 40, 41, 42, 43, 44, 45, 46, 47, 48, 49, 50, 51, 52, 53, 54, 55, 56, 57, 59, 60, 61, 62, 63, 64, 65, 66, 67, 68, 69, 70, 71, 72, 73, 74, 77, 78, 79, 80
Family stories: Canada 53
Family stories: Commonwealth 14, 18, 36 *See also* Family stories: Australia etc.
Family stories: Denmark 22, 32, 44
Family stories: Europe 11, 13, 14, 18, 80 *See also* Family stories: Britain etc.
Family stories: France 11, 14
Family stories: Germany 14
Family stories: Holland 14, 68
Family stories: India 14, 66, 70
Family stories: Italy 14, 32, 34, 53, 54, 55, 68
Family stories: Jamaica 14, 22, 29, 32, 45, 48, 49, 50, 55, 60, 66, 69, 71
Family stories: Japan 41
Family stories: Norway 14, 49, 67
Family stories: South Africa 14, 22, 31, 49, 66, 70, 71

Family stories: Sweden 14, 25, 45, 53, 64
Family stories: Switzerland 11
Family stories: United States of America 10, 11, 13, 14, 17, 18, 20, 21, 22, 24, 25, 27, 29, 30, 32, 36, 40, 43, 44, 45, 46, 47, 49, 50, 53, 54, 55, 57, 60, 64, 65, 68, 69, 70, 71, 72, 73, 74
Family stories: Middle class background 12, 15, 16, 22, 40, 41, 79
Family stories: Upper middle class background 16, 22, 39, 79
Family stories: Working class background 13, 16, 22, 39, 40, 56, 57, 61, 79
Family Tower, The 18, 31
Family unit 10, 15, 16, 18, 19, 21, 22, 24, 25, 26, 28, 29, 30, 31, 33, 34, 44, 45, 48, 49, 55, 58, 60, 67, 70, 74, 75, 76, 77, 78
Fantasy 10, 11, 13, 16, 20, 35, 49, 74, 77
Farjeon, Annabel 26, 27, 53
Farmer, Penelope 25, 35
Farmers 25
Farquharson, Martha *See* Finley, Martha
Fathers 14, 15, 16, 17, 18, 22, 23, 24, 25, 26, 27, 30, 31, 32, 33, 36, 43, 46, 59, 65, 67, 68, 71, 74
Fears 35
Festivals 54
Fiction 21, 24, 26, 30, 31, 33, 37, 44, 46, 49, 50, 55, 61, 63, 64, 69, 73
Filming 12
Finley, Martha 10, 11
Finn's Folly 65, 67
Fisher, Margery 37, 39, 60, 72
Flautists 54
Flooding 23, 59, 60
Flowering spring 54
Fly-by-night 25, 40, 55, 67, 73, 74
Food 41, 42, 45, 47, 48, 64 *See also* Meals, Menus
Forest, Antonia 16, 22, 29, 31, 32, 42, 48, 49, 50, 52, 65, 72
Foster parents 25, 67
Fox, Paula 65, 73
Friend for Frances, A 25, 28
Friends 19, 25, 34, 35, 45, 48, 55, 59, 73
Friendship 19, 35, 59, 67, 71, 74
Friis, Babbis 14, 49, 67

From the mixed-up files of Mrs Basil E Frankweiler 18, 20, 72

Games 42, 50
Gangs 62
Gardening 42
Garfield, Leon 30
Garner, Alan 13, 20, 38, 40, 44, 62, 73
Garnett, Eve 12, 31, 47, 61, 62
Gates of Bannerdale, The 52
Gebhardt, Hertha von 14
Generation gap 24, 29
Gentle heritage, The 10, 19
Germany 61
Ghana 44
Ginger and number 10 22, 59, 65, 68, 74
Ginger Pye 13
Girl from nowhere, The 14
Girl of the Limberlost, A 18
Girls 10, 19, 27, 35, 36, 47, 51, 55, 66, 67, 70, 74, 77 *See also* Daughters, Granddaughters, Sisters
Gordon, Glenda 24
Governesses 19, 26
Graham, Eleanor 12, 17, 31
Grammar schools *See* Schools, Grammar
Grandchildren 32, 36
Granddaughters 32
Grandfathers 31, 32, 69
Grandmothers 31, 32, 46, 68, 71
Grandparents 31, 32, 36, 45, 78
Grandsons 31, 32, 69
Grange at High Force, The 25, 35
Great-aunts 20, 33, 48, 62
Great gale, The 60
Green, Roger Lancelyn 78
Green laurel, The 22, 25, 27, 48, 60
Green Street 34
Grice, Frederick 33
Gripe, Maria 14, 25, 45, 46, 64
Growing summer, The 20, 23, 33, 48, 62
Guardians 30, 33
Guide dog 45, 67
Gumble's Yard 74

Hairdressers 32
Hallersage sound, The 30, 53, 70
Handicapped children *See* Children, Handicapped

Harris, Mary K 18, 19, 23, 24, 26, 27, 28, 29, 30, 32, 35, 39, 42, 46, 48, 49, 50, 51, 54, 61, 64, 68, 71, 72
Hazard, Paul 38, 39
Headmasters 51
Headmistresses 30, 51
Heidi 11
Heinemann 77
Heir of Redclyffe, The 10
Hell's Edge 19, 25, 27, 30, 70
Hentoff, Nat 53
Heroin 56
High house, The 18, 33, 70
Highwayman, The 68
Hildick, E W 35, 43, 61, 67
Hill, Janet A 15
Hills and hollows 42
Hills End 50
Hire purchase 62
Historical novels 29, 62
History of the Fairchild family, The 9, 12, 15
Hitler, Adolf 56
Hobbies 40, 42, 55, 80
Holiday House 9, 17, 52
Holidays 37, 39, 40, 45, 48, 55, 62, 79
Hollywood 12
Home 9, 12, 26, 31, 38, 39, 40, 41, 42, 43, 46, 48, 49, 51, 55, 56, 59, 61, 63, 64, 68, 76, 78, 79, 80
Homesickness 11
Homework 55
Horses 25, 55, 73
Hospitals 22, 25, 59
Hough, Charlotte 59
Housekeeping 64
Housing 27, 30, 62
How many miles to Babylon? 65, 73
Hull, Kathleen 62
Humour 23, 31, 46, 65
Hunt for Harry, The 33, 64, 66, 74
Hurricane 22, 29, 60
Hurricanes 59, 60
Hürlimann, Bettina 11

' I own the racecourse!' 67
Illegitimacy 59, 63, 66
Illness 22, 23, 24, 25, 35, 59, 67
Imagination 38, 39, 59
Immigrants 80
In-between Miya 41
In spite of all terror 62

Incomes 63
India 14, 44, 66, 70
Industrial relations 56
Inferiority 29
Inger, Nan 43, 45, 53, 64
Insecurity 63
Intent upon reading 37, 39, 60
Ireland 20
Ironmongers 22, 24
Islands of strangers 69
It's like this, cat 24, 49, 55, 68, 70, 71

Jam tomorrow 60
Jamaica 14, 44
Janáček, Leoš 53
Japan 41, 44
Jazz 53
Jazz country 53
Jealousy 28, 58, 71
Jennifer, Hecate, Macbeth and me 18, 32, 45, 65, 74
Jessica on her own 18, 24, 29, 50, 68, 71
Jews 61 *See also* Anti-semitism
Journeys 47, 60
Junior bookshelf, The 12

Kaeser, H J 13
Kamm, Josephine 32, 66
Katrin 43, 53, 64
Kersti 14, 67
Konigsburg, *Mrs* E L 14, 18, 20, 27, 30, 32, 45, 65, 72, 74
Krumgold, Joseph 14, 22, 24, 30, 71
Kullman, Harry 14

Ladder to the sky 24, 29, 60, 65, 72
Lamplighter, The 11, 52
Lamplugh, Lois 73
Lark in the morn, The 53, 78
Lark on the wing, The 53
Laski, Marghanita 16, 19
Latchkey children, The 23, 63, 64, 66, 70
Latini, Angela 14, 32, 55, 68
Launderettes 63
Laundering 13
Lavatories 22
Law 22, 23, 34, 53
Lecturers 25, 30
Lewis, Clive Staples 52
Lewis, Naomi 59

Libraries 40, 51, 52, 54, 55
Library quarterly, The 74
Library review 20
Lindgren, Astrid 14
Linhay on Hunter's Hill, The 73
Literacy 12, 68
Literature and the young child 17, 58
Little Lord Fauntleroy 11, 40
Little pretty pocket book, A 9
Little princess, A 11
Little women 10, 17, 53
Liverpool 43
Lizzie Lights 66, 67
Local government 34
Loeff, A Rutgers Van der 14, 68
London 23, 43, 47
Lord Mayor's show, The 25, 73
Lorry drivers 22, 67
Lost children *See* Children, Lost
Lunt, Alice 45, 68

Mackenzie, Compton 52
Macmillan 77
Magic stone, The 25, 35
Magnolia Buildings 32, 48, 53
Malheurs de Sophie, Les 11
Manchester 44
Margin for surprise 61
Maria Lupin 27
Marle 32
Marriage 30, 70
Mary's meadow 10
Mayne, William 13, 20, 22, 23, 25, 28, 33, 34, 35, 38, 40, 42, 43, 44, 47, 48, 49, 50, 51, 52, 53, 61, 62, 66, 73
Maythorn story, The 47
Meals 23, 38, 41, 42, 45, 55
Medicine 22
Meek, Margaret 22, 39
Meet Lemon Kelly 43
Menus 33, 41, 45
Michael, Manfred 13
Middle classes *See* Classes, Middle
Midway 24, 29, 31, 54, 64
Milan 39, 71
' Mimff ' books 13
Ministering children 10
Miracles on Maple Hill 24, 25, 46, 53, 71
Moffats, The 13, 18, 43
Molesworth, Mrs Mary Louisa 9, 10, 12, 20

Mongols 67
Montgomery, L M 53
Moral tale 9, 10, 12, 15, 17
Morality 10, 11, 15, 38, 59, 63, 77, 80
Mortuaries 22
Mothers 14, 17, 18, 23, 24, 25, 26, 27, 28, 30, 31, 33, 36, 37, 43, 45, 46, 48, 54, 64, 65, 70, 74 *See also* Working mothers
Mozart, Wolfgang Amadeus 53
Museums 45
Music 51, 53
Music, Pop 53
Musical honours 53
Musical instruments 53, 54
Mysteries 37

National Health Service 56
Neighbours 19
Nesbit, Edith 11, 12, 20
Neville, Emily Cheney 18, 22, 23, 24, 27, 30, 44, 49, 55, 60, 65, 68, 70, 71, 74
New York 48, 72
Newbery, John 9
Newbery Medal 13
Newbolt, Henry 68
Nigeria 44
' Nipper ' books 40
No boats on Bannermere 28
No one must know 73
No strangers here 32, 66, 67
Nordy Bank 26, 48, 73
Nortje, P H 14, 22, 31, 49, 66, 70, 71
Norton, Mary 52
Nurseries 13, 16

Oban 44
Observer, The 38
Offices 64
Old-fashioned girl, An 10
Old people 32, 47, 54, 59, 68, 71
Ollie 68
Onion John 22, 24, 71
Only children *See* Children, Only
Open days 50
Orphans 30, 32, 33, 36, 71
Ottley, Reginald 55, 74
Out of step 66
Outings 15, 40, 45, 46, 47, 55, 56, 65
Owl in the barn, The 59

Owl service, The 44
Oxford 52

Pair of Jesus-boots, A 13, 43
Palmer, C Everard 14, 32, 45, 55, 69, 71
Pantomimes 47
Pappa Pellerin's daughter 14, 25, 46, 64
Paradise summer, The 24, 73
Parcel of trees, A 40, 43
Parents 12, 14, 15, 16, 17, 18, 19, 21, 22, 23, 24, 26, 28, 30, 32, 33, 34, 35, 36, 37, 38, 46, 47, 48, 49, 56, 57, 58, 59, 61, 63, 64, 65, 69, 71, 72, 76, 77, 78, 80 *See also* Fathers, Mothers
Parker, Richard 26, 27, 28, 32, 60, 66, 67
Parks 45
Parties 46, 47
Pastures of the blue crane 30, 32, 48, 69
Patterson's Track 29, 48, 72
Pauline 19, 30, 35, 48, 50, 72
Pavilion, The 28, 51, 53, 78
Pearce, A Philippa 19, 20, 22, 24, 29, 31, 32, 38, 44, 46, 47, 52, 54, 55, 74
Peers 47, 48
Penny's way 24, 27, 29, 50, 64
Periodical articles 12, 14, 15, 16, 18, 20, 29, 35, 38, 39, 55, 61, 62, 66, 74
Perkins, Lucy Fitch 40
Peter's room 16, 52
Pets 40, 42, 51, 55, 59 *See also* Cats, Dogs etc.
Peyton, K M 25, 29, 30, 40, 52, 55, 60, 67, 73, 74
Phipson, Joan 22, 27, 71
Phoenix and the carpet, The 12
Pianists 54, 64
Picard, Barbara Leonie 30
Picnics 47, 48
Pierrots 47
Piers 47
Pilgrim, Anne 17, 26, 27, 28, 73
Pineapple Palace 53, 67, 69
Pinky Pye 13
Pirate's island 27, 28, 34
Plan for Birdsmarsh, The 29, 60
Plots 44, 61
Police 22

' Pony stories ' 16
Pop music *See* Music, Pop
Porter, Gene Stratton 18
Porter, Sheena 17, 22, 23, 26, 27, 28, 30, 34, 39, 42, 44, 46, 47, 48, 50, 55, 60, 62, 70, 72, 73
Portrait of Margarita 18, 30, 66, 67, 71
Presley, Elvis 56
Private beach 26, 28
Problems 14, 15, 16, 18, 19, 20, 24, 25, 26, 27, 29, 30, 33, 34, 35, 36, 37, 39, 44, 45, 48, 55, 58, 59, 60, 61, 62, 63, 64, 65, 66, 67, 68, 69, 70, 71, 73, 74, 76, 77, 80 *See also* Current issues, Racial issues
Public libraries acts 12
Publishers 14, 77 *See also* Individual publishers
Puerto Ricans 65
Pullein-Thompson, Diana 68
Purple jar, The 15

Quarrels 35, 42, 65
Questers, The 35, 67

Racial integration 56, 59, 66, 74
Racial issues 15, 31, 59, 63, 65, 71
Radio 51
Railwaymen 22
Ransome, Arthur 12, 23, 31, 52
Rasmus and the tramp 14
Rathnamal, Sita 14, 70
Ration books 56
Readers 9, 13, 15, 21, 23, 25, 26, 27, 28, 37, 39, 40, 41, 42, 44, 46, 50, 52, 53, 56, 58, 59, 66, 68, 74, 75, 80
Reading 40, 51, 52, 68
Real game, The 11, 40
Realism 12, 15, 17, 21, 22, 28, 29, 35, 38, 41, 50, 51, 55, 61, 62, 68, 70, 71, 74, 77
Reality 12, 13, 16, 18, 19, 23, 24, 26, 29, 30, 31, 33, 38, 39, 40, 42, 44, 47, 49, 50, 52, 55, 56, 58, 59, 61, 62, 63, 64, 66, 68, 69, 73, 74, 76, 77, 78, 79, 80
Redlich, Monica 60
Reggiani, Renée 14, 34, 53, 54
Relationships 14, 15, 19, 21, 23, 24, 25, 27, 28, 29, 31, 32, 33, 34, 35, 36, 44, 45, 54, 65, 66, 67, 68, 69, 70, 76, 77, 78

Relatives 18, 33, 73, 77, 78 *See also* Aunts etc.

Religion 63

Reluctant reader, The 53, 78

Remarriage 17, 28, 30, 59, 63, 65, 74

Requiem for a princess 16, 33, 66, 67

Riding 51

Robinson. Veronica 67

Rolling season, The 66

Rose in bloom 10

Rossie 68

Royal Air Force 56

Royal Society for the Prevention of Cruelty to Animals 56

Running away 61, 71, 72

Sailing 12

Sales 48

Sales of work 33, 42, 50

Salkey, Andrew 14, 22, 29, 48, 49, 50, 60, 71

Sampson's Circus 73

Sand 35, 50, 51

Sandford and Merton 9, 12, 17

Saturdays, The 13, 47, 72

Scapegoat, The 17, 70, 72

Scarlatti, Domenico 53

Scholar gipsy, The 52

Scholarships 34

School 24, 26, 29, 31, 35, 38, 39, 40, 42, 43, 46, 48, 49, 50, 51, 55, 59, 61, 62, 64, 68, 69, 74, 78, 79, 80, *See also* Schools, Boarding etc.

School librarian, The 55

School stories 49, 51, 61, 78

Schools, Boarding 13, 19, 49, 51, 79

Schools, Comprehensive 51

Schools, Grammar 12, 29, 61, 74

Schools, Secondary Modern 29, 35

Scotch twins, The 40

Scotland 40 *See also* Edinburgh, Oban

Sea peril 50

Seaside 47

Second-hand family 67

Secret garden, The 11

Security 16, 66, 72

Ségur, La Comtesse de 11

Selina's new family 17, 26, 27

Seraphina 30, 32, 46, 48, 50, 71

Servants 15, 16, 19, 20, 26, 31, 61, 63, 64

Settings, Industrial 16, 30

Seventeenth Street gang, The 65, 70, 71

Severnside story, A 33

Sex 69, 70

Shakespeare, William 52

Shanta 32, 44

Shaw, Flora 10

She shall have music 53

Sherry, Sylvia 13, 43

Sherwood, *Mrs* Martha Mary 9, 15, 17

Shopkeepers 22

Shropshire 44

Shyness 25, 70

Siblings 21, 28, 29, 30, 42, 58, 63, 64, 78

Sickness *See* Illness

Sinclair, Catherine 9, 17, 52

Sinister Street 52

Sisters 18, 20, 21, 22, 28, 29, 31, 33, 38, 40, 42, 70, 71, 72

Six to sixteen 10

Sixth-formers 52

Skating 12

Skinny 68

Slaughter houses 22

Sleigh, Barbara 73

Smith, James Steel 69

Smith, Vian 25, 73

Smoking 26

Snobbishness 16

Snow 60

Snowbound bus, The 24, 60

Sociologists 18, 41, 43, 47, 52

Songberd's Grove 28

Sons 24, 25, 27, 28, 30, 32, 36

Sorensen, Virginia 22, 24, 25, 46, 53, 71

South Africa 14, 44

Southall, Ivan 14, 19, 27, 38, 45, 50, 60, 65, 67, 69, 71

Spence, Eleanor 14, 19, 22, 23, 25, 27, 29, 37, 45, 48, 49, 53, 54, 60, 62, 71, 72, 73

Sports 40, 49, 50, 51

Spring, Howard 45, 73

Spring of the year, The 54

Spyri, Johanna 11

Steele, Tommy 56

Stepmothers 70

Stolz, Mary 23, 69

Storey, Margaret 19, 23, 30, 34, 35, 48, 49, 50, 61, 72

Strangers at the Farm School 61
Streatfeild, Noel 12, 16, 20, 23, 33, 46, 48, 50, 52, 54, 62
Stretton, Hesba 10
Stucley, Elizabeth 20, 32, 48, 53, 62
Study 38
Summer visitors 42, 48, 50
Sunday 38, 43
Sutcliff, Rosemary 30, 52
Swallows and Amazons 12
Swarm in May, A 49, 53

Tales out of school 17, 31, 39, 72
Tansy of Tring Street 73
Tasmania 14
Taylor, J K G 35, 55, 61, 62
Teachers 23, 49, 50, 71 *See also* Governesses, Tutors
Teenagers 25, 27, 30, 33, 59, 63, 66, 67, 69, 70, 76, 77
Television 23, 43, 56
Tellers of tales 78
Tennis 12
Tessie growing up 73
Theatres 45
Thimble summer 13
Thøger, Marie 22, 32, 44
Three and one to carry 70
Three centuries of children's books in Europe 11
Thursday kidnapping, The 48, 72
Times literary supplement 18, 66
Timpetill 13
To the wild sky 19, 27
Tomalin, Claire 38
Toppling Towers, The 31, 56
Towns 30, 34, 44, 48
Townsend, John Rowe 12, 14, 19, 20, 23, 25, 26, 27, 28, 29, 30, 33, 34, 47, 51, 53, 57, 60, 62, 69, 70, 74
Tractarians 10
Trade 34
Translations 11, 13, 14, 36, 80
Treadgold, Mary 27, 28, 44, 47, 62, 64
Trease, Geoffrey 17, 22, 28, 31, 39, 42, 47, 50, 52, 54, 60, 72
Tumbledown Dick 45
Turner, Philip 23, 25, 30, 34, 35, 41, 44, 49, 50, 67
Tutors 17
Twain, Mark 18
Twentieth century children's books 16, 39

Twins 31
Two sisters, The 24, 69

Uchida, Yoshiko 41
Uncles 33, 36, 46, 71
Under the lilacs 10
Unemployment 38, 71
United Nations Organisation 56
United States of America 44, 64, 68
University of London Press 14
Upper middle classes *See* Classes, Upper middle

Victorian tales for girls 16, 19
Vietnam 56
Viguers, Ruth Hill 61
Violinists 54
Vipont, Elfrida 28, 42, 45, 51, 53, 54, 78
Visitors 38
Visitors from London 62
Visits 55, 56
Von Schweinitz, Eleanor 74

Wales 44
Walsh, Jill Paton 57, 62
Warner, Priscilla M 24, 25, 28, 73
Wayne, Jenifer 22, 26, 40, 55, 64, 68
We couldn't leave Dinah 62
We'll meet in England 62
Weddings 29
Weekends 55
Weir, Rosemary 11, 33, 40, 64, 66, 74
Welfare State 10
West Indians 22, 66, 74
Wetherell, Elizabeth 11, 18
What Katy did 11, 17
What Katy did at school 11
Whitlock, Pamela 62
Who's who of children's literature, The 13
Widdershins Crescent 47, 74
Wide, wide world, The 11, 18
Widowers 17, 25, 28, 59
Widows 18, 26, 28, 59
Wild goose summer 31, 49, 66, 70
Willard, Barbara 17, 18, 22, 26, 28, 30, 31, 33, 34, 42, 45, 46, 47, 49, 50, 56, 60, 70, 72, 73, 78
Willson, Robina Beckles 53, 67, 69
Wilson library bulletin 14, 29

Wiltshire 66
Winter princess, The 28, 47, 64
Wish fulfilment 17, 30, 31, 38, 49, 51, 55, 58, 61, 71
Wives 66, 69
Work 43, 69 *See also* Employment
Working classes *See* Classes, Working
Working mothers 23, 26, 31, 59, 62, 63, 64, 70
World War 2 25, 33, 62, 71

Wrightson, Patricia 67
Writing 26, 52
Written for children 12, 69

Year of the currawong, The 37, 54
Yonge, Charlotte M 9, 10
Yorkshire 44

Za the truffle boy 14, 32, 55, 68
Zoos 45
Zweigbergk, Eva von 16

DATE DUE

DEC 1 1982	
DEC 8 1982	